Patterns for Pooches

Patterns for Pooches

Anne Burton

Photographs by Michael and Anne Burton

NEW HOLLAND

Author's Acknowlegements

Thank you first and foremost to my husband Michael Burton for his continual love and support (and for letting me put our dog in a bonnet). Thanks also to Larry Gawel, the Holz family, Wendy Weiss, Jay Kreimer, Kim and Mark Thomas, Marissa Vigneault, Bill Graham and Peggy Gomez for their assistance with this project. Finally, I am most grateful to our adorable furry models Calvin, Hannah, Bare, Jet, Max, Archie, Rocco, Rosie, Bean and Lily. Thanks for humouring us!

First published in 2013 by
New Holland Publishers
London • Sydney • Cape Town • Auckland
www.newhollandpublishers.com • www.newholland.com.au

Garfield House 86–88 Edgware Road London W2 2EA United Kingdom
1/66 Gibbes Street Chatswood NSW 2067 Australia
Wembley Square First Floor Solan Road Gardens Cape Town 8001 South Africa
218 Lake Road Northcote Auckland New Zealand

A catalogue record of this book is available at the British Library and at the National Library of Australia

ISBN: 9781742572550

10 9 8 7 6 5 4 3 2 1

Publisher: Fiona Schultz
Editor: Simona Hill
Designer: Tracy Loughlin
Cover Design: Kimberley Pearce
Photographer: Anne and Michael Burton
Production director: Olga Dementiev
Printer: Toppan Leefung Printing Limited

10 9 8 7 6 5 4 3 2 1

Follow New Holland Publishers on
Facebook: www.facebook.com/NewHollandPublishers

Contents

Introduction

The summer my husband and I got married we brought home a Boston terrier puppy and named him Bean. Our sweet little Bean was a handful from the start, full of personality and in the middle of everything all the time. As a first-time pet owner, I learned a lot in those first few months and was quickly in love with our new furry family member.

When the weather started to cool and the Nebraska wind began to blow, Bean was not shy about his lack of enthusiasm for the cold. He would hide under blankets and try to crawl under our sweaters. I decided to crochet him a sweater in the hopes it would stay on and keep him warm and comfortable. Having learned to crochet in a college sculpture class, I only knew a few basic stitches but I found the challenge of designing for Bean really exciting.

Over the next few months I kept revising my dog sweater design. I created ten sweaters for Bean and more sweaters for every dog of every shape and size we knew. Pretty soon a small business was born and I started selling customized dog sweaters, scarves and hats over the internet, at craft shows, and to pet boutiques around the world. I've created sweaters for 2 lb chihuahuas and 200 lb great danes. I've also created a lot of items just for fun, taking full advantage of Bean's natural modelling ability and his enthusiasm for being in front of the camera. A few years ago we adopted a second Boston terrier, Lily, from a rescue centre, who has truly filled out our pack. Bean and Lily are featured modeling many of the patterns in this book.

I would describe my design style as simple and practical with a quirky sense of humour. I use crochet because it is a versatile medium that can be easily modified and customized. Throughout this book I'll offer sizing options and instructions on how to tailor an item to give your pet the best fit possible. I use basic crochet stitches, and all of these patterns are for beginners to intermediate levels.

The better an item fits, the less it will inhibit your pet's natural movement. I strive to create pieces that animals won't mind, or better yet, won't be aware they have on. I hope you'll enjoy creating these items for the pooches in your life. For all the unconditional affection they give us, pets deserve our love, respect, and a cosy sweater or scarf.

Crochet Basics

Standard abbreviations

Ch	Chain
Dc	Double crochet
Dec	Decrease (skip a stitch)
Inc	Increase (create two stitches in one stitch)
Lp(s)	Loop
Sc	Single crochet
Sl st	Slip stitch
Sk	Skip
Tr	Treble crochet
BL	Back loop
FL	Front loop
YO	Yarn over
Rem	Remaining
*	repeat the instructions between the asterisks

I have written this book for readers around the world, so patterns include both UK and US stitch names and measurements. Please refer to this conversion chart before starting the patterns to make sure you are familiar with the similarities and differences between the stitch names. Where stitch names differ, I have included both separated with an oblique symbol. The UK stitch names appear first.

Stitch conversion chart

UK/AUS Term =	= US Term
Sc single crochet	= Sl st slip stitch
Dc double crochet	= Sc single crochet
Htr half treble crochet	= Hdc half double crochet
Tr treble crochet	= Dc double crochet
Dtr double treble crochet	= Tr treble crochet

The patterns in this book are worked with a few basic stitches and techniques. If you are new to crochet, then practise first so that you can crochet at a consistent tension. Most people tend to hold the hook with their dominant hand, and the yarn with their non-dominant hand.

A crochet stitch has a main body and a top that appears like a V shape with the two loops. The main body of the stitch is called the post.

Slipknot

A slipknot is the first step in beginning most crochet projects. Leaving around 15 cm (6 in) of yarn as a tail, wrap the yarn around your finger to make a loop. Take this loop and fold it on top of the yarn under the tail. Pull this yarn through the loop and put your crochet hook through it. Pull the tail to tighten the yarn around the hook.

Creating a chain (Ch)

Beginning with a slipknot, wrap yarn over the hook from the back to the front. This is called a **yarn over (yo)**. Catch the yarn with the crook (end of the hook) and pull it through the slipknot. You have created the first loop in your chain. Yarn over again and pull this loop through the loop you just created in your chain to create another stitch. Repeat until you have as many stitches in your chain as the pattern indicates.

Every stitch except the slipknot counts as a chain stitch in your chain.

Double crochet/Single crochet (dc/sc)

This stitch is called double crochet in the UK and single crochet in the United States. Everything about the stitch is the same except for the name. In patterns I refer to this stitch as dc/sc to allow for readers from all English-speaking countries to use the stitch names they are familiar with.

Insert your hook under both loops of the second chain from your hook. Yarn over and pull the loop through the stitch. You now have two loops on your hook. Yarn over again and pull the loop through both loops on your hook. You have now completed the double crochet/single crochet stitch.

To begin double (single) crochet from a chain stitch, put the hook under the loop in the second chain from the hook. Yarn and over and pull the yarn through the loop. You now have two loops on your hook. Yarn over again and pull the loop through both loops on your hook. You have now completed the double crochet/ single crochet stitch.

Slip stitch (sl st)

Slip stitch is a tight, small stitch that is commonly used to join pieces of crochet or to move from one part of a row to another.

Insert the hook into the next stitch. Yarn over and then pull the yarn through the stitch and the loop on the hook. This is one slip stitch.

Half treble crochet/Half double crochet (htr/hdc)

To begin a project with a row of htr/hdc, create a foundation chain with the number of stitches you require plus 2. Begin htr/hdc in the third chain from the hook. Your ch 2 counts as the first stitch.

Yarn over once, insert hook into next stitch and yarn over then draw the yarn through the stitch. You now have three loops on the hook. Yarn over and pull the yarn through all three loops. You now have 1 loop left on the hook and have completed your first htr/ hdc. Continue until the end of the row, ch 2 and turn. Begin your next row of htr/hdc in the second stitch from the hook. The ch 2 counts as the first stitch in the row.

Treble crochet/Double crochet (tr/dc)

To begin a project with a row of tr/dc, create a foundation chain with the number of stitches you require plus three. Begin tr/dc in the fourth chain from the hook. Your ch 3 counts as the first stitch.

Yarn over one time. Insert the hook into the next stitch, yarn over and pull the yarn through the stitch. Three loops are now on the hook.

Yarn over again and pull the yarn through the first two loops on the hook. Yarn over and pull the yarn through the remaining two loops. You have now made one treble crochet/double crochet stitch. At the end of the row, chain three and turn. Being the next row in the second stitch from the hook. The chain 3 counts as the first stitch in the row.

Double crochet/treble crochet (dtr/tr)

Double treble crochet/treble crochet is a tall stitch that makes projects go quickly. Begin your foundation chain with the number of stitches you require plus four. Yarn over twice and insert the yarn in the fifth chain from the hook. Yarn over and draw the yarn through the stitch. You now have four loops on the hook.

Yarn over and draw the hook through two of the loops. Yarn over again and draw the hook through two loops. Yarn over a third time and draw the hook through the remaining two loops. You now have one loop remaining and have completed one dtr/tr stitch.

Front loop only (flo)

Work stitch in loop closest to you.

Back Loop Only (blo)

Work in the loop furthest from you.

Which crochet hook size for which yarn?

Hook size	Yarn weight	Yarn types
2.25–3.5 mm	Super Fine	Baby, Sock, Fingering, Lace-weight, 2ply
3.5–4.5 mm	Fine	Baby, Sport, 4 ply
4.5–5.5 mm	Light	DK, Light Worsted, 8 ply
5.5–6.5 mm	Medium	Worsted, Afghan, Aran, 10 ply, 12 ply
6.5–9 mm	Bulky	Chunky, Craft, Rug, 14 ply
9 mm	Super Bulky	Bulky, Roving and larger

Crochet hook sizes

The gauge you achieve when crocheting depends on the hook size you use and the yarn weight. This hook size translation chart will help in reading crochet patterns from around the world.

Metric	USA	UK/AUS/CAN
2 mm	–	14
2.25 mm	B/1	13
2.5 mm	–	12
2.75 mm	C/2	–
3 mm	–	11
3.25 mm	D/3	10
3.5 mm	E/4	9
3.75 mm	F/5	-
4 mm	G/6	8
4.5 mm	7	7
5 mm	H/8	6
5.5 mm	I/9	5
6 mm	J/10	4
6.5 mm	K/10.5	3
7 mm	L/11	2
8 mm	M/13	0
9 mm	N/14	00
10 mm	P	000
16 mm	Q/16	-

Yarn weights

Yarn weight classifies the thickness of a strand of yarn. The majority of the projects in this book are created with medium-weight, bulky and super-bulky yarns, which are the most durable for the wear and tear they endure on your pet. Bulkier yarns also make for easy projects that come together quickly.

Hat sizes

The neck circumference is taken at the base of the head. Breeds with large round heads, similar to French bulldogs and pugs, may need a medium or large hat. Dogs with narrow heads such as dobermans and labradors usually fit a medium hat.

Size	Neck circumference	Ear hole circumference	Distance between ears
X small breeds	Chihuahua, Yorkie, miniature pinscher, toy poodle, papillon, silky terrier		
	18–25 cm/7–10 in	14 cm/5½ in	6 cm/2½ in
Small breeds	Boston terrier, French bulldog, Pekingese, small pug, Jack Russell, Scottish terrier, West Highland terrier, Australian terrier		
	28–35 cm/11–14 in	15 cm/6 in	9 cm /3½ in
Medium breeds	Large Boston terrier, large French bulldog, beagle, medium to large pug, small labrador or golden retriever, cocker spaniel, doberman, greyhound		
	35–43 cm/14–17 in	15 cm/6 in	10 cm/4 in
Large breeds	Bulldog, golden retriever, pitbull terrier, boxer, poodle, Bernese mountain dog		
	45–56 cm/18–22 cm	16.5 cm/6½ in	13 cm/5 in

Sweater sizes

Dogs can vary widely in their proportions. To create a longer body or rump for the sweater, add one row of dc/sc to add roughly 2.5 cm (1 in) to the length of the chest or rump. If your pet's belly tapers in at the waist, decrease approximately 5 stitches in the last 3–4 rows of the belly. Whippets, dobermans and similar dogs with a large chest and very small girth may decrease as much as 8 stitches through the belly.

Most dogs and cats prefer not to have their sweater close to their tail. Though you may want to add length to some of the patterns to keep their rump warm, make sure the sweater length will not brush the base of their tail.

Many of these sweaters are created with a bulky or super-bulky-weight yarn. Allow for about 2.5–10 cm (1–4 in) of stretch with regular wear when using chunky weight yarns.

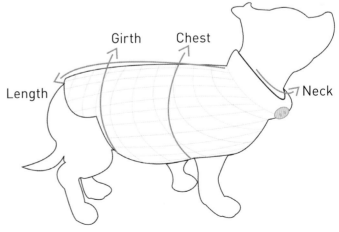

Irresistible Hats

Top Hat

For the discerning pet, only a top hat will do for fancy dress. This crocheted hat is created in three pieces and reinforced inside with flexible chipboard. Measure the circumference from the neck around the top of your pet's head to work out the size of the chinstrap.

Skill level: Intermediate

Materials
Crochet hook size: 9 mm (N/14, 00)
Yarn: Super-bulky weight, cotton, acrylic
    or wool, 27.5 m (30 yd)
Flexible chipboard
Hot glue gun and glue
Felt, 44 x 28 cm (17 x 11 in)
Fabric glue
Needle and thread

1 cm (½ in)-wide elastic
    For extra small, 15–23 cm (6–9 in)
    For small, 23–30 cm (9–12 in)
    For medium, 30–38 cm (12–16 in)
    For large, 38–51 cm (16–20 in)
1 cm (½ in)-wide satin ribbon, 18 cm (7 in)
    of plus extra to make a bow

Gauge 10 sts = 10 cm (4 in)
1 row tr/dc = (approximately)
    2 cm (¾ in) high

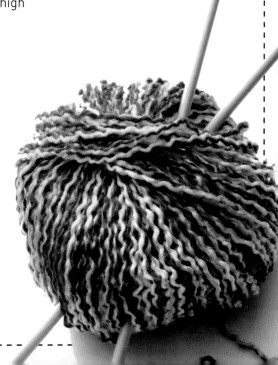

HAT TOP

Ch 3 and join in a loop.
Dc/sc 5 in circle and join to last stitch in ch 3.
Ch 1 and turn.
Row 1: Dc/sc, dc/sc and inc 1 (dc/sc again once in same stitch), dc/sc 2, dc/sc inc 1, dc/sc in last stitch and join in loop (total of dc/sc 8).
Ch 1 and turn.
Row 2: Dc/sc 3, dc/sc and inc 1, dc/sc 2, dc/sc and inc 1, dc/sc, dc/sc in last stitch (total of dc/sc 11).
Tie off.

HAT SIDES

Ch 15 and join in circle.
Dc/sc 5 rows and tie off.

HAT BASE

Ch 3 and join in circle.
Dc/sc 4 in circle and join.
Ch 1 and turn.
Row 1: Dc/sc, dc/sc and inc 1, dc/sc, dc/sc and inc 1, dc/sc in last st and join in loop (total of dc/sc 7).
Ch 1 and turn.
Row 2: Dc/sc 3, dc/sc and inc 1, dc/sc 2, dc/sc and inc 1, dc/sc in last st (total of dc/sc 10).
Ch 1 and turn.
Row 3: Dc/sc 3, dc/sc and inc 1, dc/sc 3, dc/sc and inc 1, dc/sc 2, dc/sc and inc 1 (total of dc/sc 15).
Row 4: Dc/sc around circle, dc/sc and inc 1 in last stitch.
Tie off.

MAKING UP

Cut the hat body and hat base from chipboard.
Form the hat body piece into a tube and hot glue as indicated on the pattern.
Using the templates provided cut 1 hat body, 1 hat top and 2 hat bases from felt.
Using fabric glue, stick the felt hat body to the chipboard, then glue one hat top and one hat base to one side of the appropriate chipboard piece. Set aside the second felt hat base.
Slide the hat body piece into the crocheted hat body. Use a small amount of hot glue or fabric glue to stick these together.
Use fabric glue to stick the felt side of the hat top to the wrong side of the crocheted hat top.
Stick the felt-covered hat base to the wrong side of the crocheted hat base in the same way.
Place the hat top on the hat body and whip stitch the crocheted edges together.
Squeeze hot glue along the inside seam of the hat top and body to reinforce them.
Put a bead of fabric glue on the bottom rim of the hat body. Place hat body on the hat base and leave to dry. Whip stitch the crocheted body and hat base pieces together.
Use hot glue to attach the elastic to each side of the underside of the hat base.
Use fabric glue to cover the underside of the hat base then stick the remaining felt piece on top.
Whip stich the felt to the crochet around the edge.
Wrap the ribbon around the body of the hat overlapping slightly at the end, and attach it with a small bead of fabric glue.
Glue the bow over the overlap.

Blue Blossom Tie-String Hat

This whimsical bonnet ties with a string and is topped with a large blue two-tone flower. Since it is made with a chunky yarn, this hat is very quick to crochet. Your pup will be looking adorable for spring photos in no time at all. Be sure to give them a biscuit and a scratch if they are a good sport about it!

Skill level: Intermediate

Materials
Crochet hook size: 10 mm (P, 000) for the hat and 6 mm (J/10, 4) for the flower
Yarn colour A: Super bulky (6) for the hat base
    Extra small, 18.5 m (20 yd)
    Small, 23 m (25 yd)
    Medium, 27.5 m (30 yd)
    Large, 32 m (35 yd)
Yarn colour B: Medium-weight (4) for the flower outer, 8.25 m (9 yd)

Yarn colour C: Medium-weight (4) for the flower inner, 8.25 m (9 yd)
Yarn colour D: Medium-weight (4) for the trim, 4.5–9 m (5–10 yd)
Sewing needle and thread

Gauge 10 sts = 10 cm (4 in)
1 row tr/dc = approximately 2 cm (¾ in) high

EXTRA SMALL HAT

Leaving 15 cm/6 in of yarn end for the hat tie, ch 17.
Row 1: Tr/dc in fourth ch from hook and tr/dc 15 across row, ch 3 and turn (first ch 3 counts as stitch for total tr/dc 16).
Continue to turn after each row unless stated otherwise.
Row 2: Tr/dc 15 across row (16 total tr/dc).
Row 3: Sl st, tr/dc 13, sl st.
Row 4: Sl st, tr/dc 12, sl st.
Row 5: Sl st, ch 7, sk 3 and sl in fourth st (earhole), tr/dc 3 between ears, ch 7, sk 3 and sl in fourth st (other earhole), sl st.
Row 6: Sl st, dc/sc 2, sk 1, dc/sc 1, sk 1, dc/sc 2, tr/dc 3, dc/sc 2, dc/sc 2, sk 1, dc/sc 1, sk 1, dc/sc 2, sl st.
Row 7: Dc/sc 13, sl st 4 (1 in last sl st and sl st 3 down side of hat).
Row 8: Sl st 4 (back up side of hat), dc/sc 15, sl st 3 down opposite side of hat.
Tie off, leaving 15 cm (6 in) of yarn for hat tie.

SMALL HAT

Leaving 18 cm (7 in) of yarn end for string tie, ch 20.
Row 1: Tr/dc in fourth ch from hook and tr/dc 18 across row, ch 3 and turn (first ch 3 counts as stitch for total tr/dc 19).
Continue to turn after each row unless stated otherwise.
Row 2: Tr/dc 18 across row (total tr/dc 19).
Row 3: Sl st, tr/dc 16, sl st.
Row 4: Sl st, tr/dc 15, sl st.
Row 5: Sl st, ch 8, sk 4 and sl st in fifth st (earhole), tr/dc 4 between ears, ch 8, sk 4 and sl st in fifth st (other earhole), sl st.
Row 6: Sl st, dc/sc 2, sk 1, dc/sc 2, sk 1, dc/sc 2, tr/dc 4, dc/sc 2, sk 1, dc/sc 2, sk 1, dc/sc 2, sl st.
Row 7: Dc/sc 16, sl st 6 (1 in last sl st and 5 sl st down side of hat).
Row 8: Sl st 5 (back up side of hat), dc/sc 18, sl st 3 down opposite side of hat.
Tie off, leaving 18 cm (7 in) of yarn for hat tie.

MEDIUM HAT

Leaving 18 cm (7 in) yarn on end for hat tie, ch 23.
Row 1: Tr/dc in fourth ch from hook and tr/dc 21 across row, ch 3 and turn (first ch 3 counts as stitch for 22 total tr/dc).
Continue to turn after each row unless stated otherwise.
Row 2: Tr/dc 21 across row (total tr/dc 22).
Row 3: Sl st, tr/dc 19, sl st.
Row 4: Sl st, tr/dc 18, sl st.
Row 5: Sl st, tr/dc 1, ch 8, sk 4 and sl st in fifth st (earhole), tr/dc 5 between ears, ch 8, sk 4 and sl st in fifth st (other earhole), tr/dc 1, sl st.
Row 6: Sl st, dc/sc 2, sk 1, dc/sc 2, sk 1, dc/sc 2, tr/dc 4, dc/sc 2, sk 1, dc/sc 2, sk 1, dc/sc 3, sl st.
Row 7: Dc/sc 17, sl st 6 (1 in last sl st and sl st 5 down side of hat).
Row 8: Sl st 5 (back up side of hat), dc/sc 19, sl st 3 down opposite side of hat.
Tie off, leaving 18 cm (7 in) for hat tie.

LARGE HAT

Leaving 20 cm (8 in) yarn on end for hat tie, ch 25.
Row 1: Tr/dc in fourth ch from hook and tr/dc 24 across row, ch 3 and turn (first ch 3 counts as stitch for total tr/dc 25).
Continue to turn after each row unless stated otherwise.
Row 2: Tr/dc 24 across row (25 total tr/dc).
Row 3: Sl st, tr/dc 22, sl st.
Row 4: Sl st, tr/dc 21, sl st.
Row 5: Sl st, tr/dc 1, ch 9, sk 5 and sl st in sixth st (earhole), tr/dc 5 between ears, ch 9, sk 5 and sl st in sixth st (other earhole), tr/dc 1, sl st.
Row 6: Sl st, dc/sc 2, sk 1, dc/sc 3, sk 1, dc/sc 2, tr/dc 5, dc/sc 2, sk 1, dc/sc 3, sk 1, dc/sc 3, sl st.
Row 7: Dc/sc 19, sl st 6 (1 in last sl st and sl st 5 down side of hat).
Row 8: Sl st 5 (back up side of hat), dc/sc 21, sl st 3 down opposite side of hat.

Tie off, leaving 20 cm (8 in) for string tie.

HAT TRIM

Hook size: 6 mm (J/10, 4)
Using medium-weight yarn,start in a corner of the
hat by the string tie and dc/sc around entire edge
of hat once for border.
Tie off and weave in ends.

BLOSSOM BASE

Ch 5 and join in ring.
Htrc/hdc 6 in ring.
Ch 5, sl st in fl, ch 5, sl st in fl around ring.
Ch 5, sl st in bl, ch 5, sl st in bl around ring.
Tie off ends.

BLOSSOM INNER

Ch 4 in ring.
Htrc/hdc 5 in ring.
Ch 4, sl st in fl, ch 4, sl st in fl around ring.
Ch 4, sl st in bl, ch4, sl st in bl around ring.
Tie off ends.
Nest blossom inner in the base and sew together.
Place blossom between ears and hand sew in place.

Pom Pom Hat with Button Strap

The open weave of the chunky crochet is perfect for the button strap on this hat, since the holes make perfect buttonholes. The hat is worked in easy-to-master single and double crochet stitches, and the neck strap can be made to measure by increasing or decreasing the stitches to the desired length. Use a pom pom maker to create the final flourish and top the hat with an adorable touch.

Skill level: Easy

Materials
Crochet hook sizes: 10 mm (P, 000);
    6 mm (J/10, 4)
Yarn: Super bulky (6)
    Extra small, 23 m (25 yd)
    Small, 32 m (35 yd)
    Medium, 36.5 m (40 yd)
    Large, 41.5 m (45 yd)
Colour B: Medium-weight (4),
    2–3 m (yd) for trim and 13 m (14 yd) for
    pom pom

2 buttons, each 25 mm (1 in) diameter
Sewing needle and thread
Pom pom maker

Gauge 10 sts = 10 cm (4 in)
1 row tr/dc = (approximately)
    2 cm (¾ in) high

Note When working in rows, turn after each row unless stated otherwise.

EXTRA SMALL HAT
Using hook size 10 mm (P, 000) ch 21.
Row 1–2: Tr/dc 18 (total 19 tr/dc including first ch 3 from end of ch).
Row 3: Sl st, tr/dc 12 across then sl st leaving 4 on end.
Row 4: Sl st, ch 7 and sk 3, sl st, tr/dc 3, ch 7, sk 3 and sl st 2.
Row 5: Sl st, dc/sc 2, sk 1, dc/sc 1, sk 1, dc/sc 2, tr/dc 3 between ears, dc/sc 2, sk 1, dc/sc 1, sk 1, dc/sc 2, sl st.
Row 6: Dc/sc 13, sl st.
Row 7: Dc/sc 13, sl st.
Row 8: Dc/sc 13, sl st and tie off.

SMALL HAT
Ch 26.
Row 1–3: Tr/dc 23 (total tr/dc 24 including first ch 3).
Row 4: Sl st, tr/dc 16, sl st, leaving 5 for strap.
Row 5: Sl st, tr/dc 15, sl st.
Row 6: Sl st, ch 8, sk 4 and sl st in fifth st (earhole), tr/dc 4 between ears, ch 8, sk 4 and sl st in fifth st (other earhole), sl st.
Row 7: Sl st, dc/sc 2, sk 1, dc/sc 2, sk 1, dc/sc 2, tr/dc 4, dc/sc 2, sk 1, dc/sc 2, sk 1, dc/sc 2, sl st.
Row 8: Sl st, tr/dc 16, sl st.
Row 9: Sl st, tr/dc 15, sl st and tie off.

MEDIUM HAT
Ch 30.
Row 1–3: Tr/dc 27 (total tr/dc 28 including first ch 3).
Row 4: Sl st, tr/dc 19, sl st, leaving 5 for strap.
Row 5: Sl st, tr/dc 18, sl st.
Row 6: Sl st, tr/dc 1, ch 8, sk 4 and sl st in fifth st (earhole), tr/dc 5 between ears, ch 8, sk 4 and sl in fifth st (other earhole), tr/dc 1, sl st.
Row 7: Sl st, dc/sc 2, sk 1, dc/sc 2, sk 1, dc/sc 2, tr/dc 4, dc/sc 2, sk 1, dc/sc 2, sk1, dc/sc 3, sl st.

Row 8: Sl st, tr/dc 18, sl st.
Row 9: Sl st, tr/dc 17, sl st and tie off.

LARGE HAT
Ch 32.
Row 1–3: Tr/dc 29 (total 30 tr/dc including first ch 3).
Row 4: Sl st, tr/dc 22, sl st, leaving 5 for strap.
Row 5: Sl st, tr/dc 21, sl st.
Row 6: Sl st, tr/dc 1, ch 9, sk 5 and sl st in sixth st (earhole), tr/dc 5 between ears, ch 9, sk 5 and sl in sixth st (other earhole), tr/dc 1, sl st.
Row 7: Sl st, dc/sc 2, sk 1, dc/sc 3, sk 1, dc/sc 2, tr/dc 5, dc/sc 2, sk 1, dc/sc 3, sk 1, dc/sc 3, sl st.
Row 8: Sl st, tr/dc 20, sl st.
Row 9: Sl st, tr/dc 19, sl st and tie off.

TRIM
Using hook size 6 mm (J/10, 4) and medium-weight yarn, dc/sc around hat to create trim.

Finishing
Sew two buttons opposite the strap and use the openweave of the crochet as buttonholes. Place one button at the base of the hat 1.25 cm (½ in) from the back edge and a second one about 5 cm (2 in) and the same distance from the back edge of the hat. Use the pom pom maker to create a pom pom for the top of the hat, and stitch into place with a needle and thread.

The Blue Baron

A cosy cap that will keep your pup's ears, head and neck warm and dry. This hood-style hat has a built-in scarf to keep your dog toasty and stylish in the great outdoors.

Skill level: Easy

Materials
Crochet hook size: 5 mm (H/8, 6)
Yarn colour A: Medium-weight (4) for hat
base
Extra small, 36.5 m (40 yd)
Small, 50 m (55 yd)
Medium, 64 m (70 yd)
Large ,82 m (90 yd)
Yarn colour B: Medium-weight (4) for hat
trim
Extra small, 9 m (10 yd)
Small, 14 m (15 yd)
Medium, 18 m (20 yd)
Large, 22.5 m (25 yd)
Sewing needle and thread
2 Buttons, each 1.25 cm (½ in)

Gauge 16 sts = 10 cm (4 in)

Finished hat size (neck circumference)
Extra small   18–28 cm (7–11 in)
Small   28–36 cm (11–14 in)
Medium   36–46 cm (14–18 in)
Large   43–51 cm (17–20 in)

Instructions are written for the Extra small size with Small, Medium, Large presented in brackets.

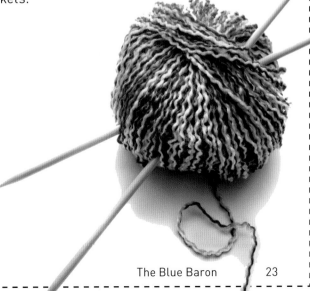

After row 20 do not turn work.
Row 21: Sl st 15 down side of hat, turn and sl st 15 up side of hat and sl st across top of hat, sl st 13 down opposite side of hat to strap, dc/sc 24 across the strap and tie off.

With colour B dc/sc around outside of entire hat. Try the hat on your pet to see how snug the neck should be. Attach buttons to the hat base to achieve the best fit for your pet's neck size. Place the buttons approximately 6 cm (2½ in) apart along the neckline of the hat.

ALL SIZES
Ch 46 (58, 74, 82).
Row 1: *Tr/dc 44 (56, 72, 80) across row, ch 3 and turn*.
Row 2: *Repeat.
Row 3: Tr/dc 4 (5, 5, 7), ch 2, sk 2, tr/dc 3 (4, 4, 5), dc 2, sk 2, tr/dc 3 (4, 4, 5), ch 2, sk 2, tr/dc 27 (38, 54, 58) across row, ch 3 and turn.
Row 4: Sl st, sc/dc 1, tr/dc 22 (33, 49, 53), dc/sc 1, sl st, turn.
Row 5: Sl st, tr/dc 21 (32, 48, 52), dc/sc 1, sl st, turn.
Row 6: *Sl st, tr/dc across, dc/sc 1 in second to last st, sl st in sl st of last row, turn*.
Rows 7–12: *Repeat.

EXTRA SMALL
After row 12 do not turn work.
Row 13: Sl st 8 down side of hat, turn and sl st 8 up side of hat and across top of hat, sl st 4 down opposite side of hat to strap, dc/sc 17 across the strap and tie off.

MEDIUM
Rows 13–16: *Repeat.
After row 16 do not turn work.
Row 17: Sl st 11 down side of hat, turn and sl st 11 up side of hat and across top of hat, sl st 7 down opposite side of hat to strap, dc/sc 20 across the strap and tie off.

LARGE
Rows 13–20: *Repeat.

Teddy Bear Hat

This soft and snuggly hood will keep ears warm and dry on winter walks. Warning: seeing your adorable dog in this hat may elicit squeals of extreme joy.

Skill level: Intermediate

Materials
Crochet hook size: 6.5 mm (K/10.5, 3)
Yarn A medium-weight: for hat body and
ear outer
Extra small, 100 m (110 yd)
Small ,119 m (130 yd)
Medium, 128 m (140 yd)
Large, 137 m (150 yd)
Yarn colour B: medium-weight for inner
ear, 18 m (20 yd)
Sewing needle and thread

Gauge 12 sts = 10 cm (4 in)

Finished hat size (neck circumference)
Extra small, 22 cm (8½ in)
Small,   29 cm (11½ in)
Medium,   35 cm (14 in)
Large,   43 cm (17 in)

Note Extra small and Small will stretch by 5 cm (2 in), Medium and Large by 9–10 cm (3½-4 in). A slightly snug fit is best so this hat will stay over your pet's ears. Increase or decrease 3–4 sts to add or remove 2.5 cm (1 in) from/to neck circumference.

Instructions are written for the Extra small size with (Small, Medium, Large) presented in brackets

HAT BODY

Ch 30 (45, 50, 58) and join in a ring.

Round 1: Ch 3 and tr/dc 27 (42, 47, 55), join in ring, ch 3 and turn (total tr/dc 28, 43, 48, 56).

Note: Continue to turn after every row unless stated otherwise.

Rounds 2–13: Tr/dc 12 (14, 15, 16) rows (ch 3 and turn at end of each tr/dc row).

Note: In the next 3 rounds, you are making the opening of the hat slightly smaller each round so it will hug the face.

Round 14 (15, 16, 17): Tr/dc 13 (22, 24, 28), dec 1, tr/dc 14 (21, 23, 27).

Round 15 (16, 17, 17): Tr/dc 12 (21, 23, 27), dec 1, tr/dc 13 (20, 22, 26).

Round 16 (17, 18, 19): Tr/dc 11 (20, 22, 26), dec 1, tr/dc 12 (19, 21, 25).

Tie off.

EARS

With colour B, ch 3 and join in a ring.

Round 1: Dc/sc 5 in ring.

Round 2: Dc/sc 1, dc/sc 2 in one st (inc 1), dc/sc 1, dc/sc 2 in one st, dc/sc 1 (dc/sc 7).

Round 3: Dc/sc 2, dc/sc 2 in 1 st, dc/sc 1, dc/sc 2 in 1 st, dc/sc 2 (dc/sc 9).

Round 4: Dc/sc 2, dc/sc 2 in 1 st, dc/sc 2, dc/sc 2 in 1 st, dc/sc 3 (dc/sc 11). Tie off.

Round 5: Rejoin colour A anywhere on colour B circle, dc/sc 1, dc/sc 2 in 1 st, dc/sc 2 in one st, dc/sc 2, dc/sc 2 in 1 st, dc/sc 2 in 1 st, dc/sc 1 (12 dc/sc), turn.

Note: The 4-stitch gap at the bottom of the circle is where you will attach the ear to the hat.

Round 6: Dc/sc 2, dc/sc 2 in 1 st, dc/sc 2 in 1 st, dc/sc 4, dc/sc 2 in 1 st, dc/sc 2 in 1 st, dc/sc 2 (dc/sc 16)

Turn and dc/sc around increasing 4 and tie off. Sew ears with open side to hat using needle and thread.

Shark Fin

A menacing fin is lurking nearby, but don't fear – this menace is pretty soft and cuddly! Tiny rows of chrocheted teeth adorn this hood-style hat that will protect little ears from the cold.

Skill level: Intermediate

Materials
Crochet hook size: 9 mm (N, 00) and
   6mm (J, 4)
Yarn: Super bulky (6), 46 m (50 yd)
   Medium-weight (4), 4.5 m (5 yd)

Gauge 10 sts = 10 cm (4 in)
1 row tr/dc = approximately
   2 cm (¾ in) high

HAT BASE

Ch 24 (28, 36, 40) and join in a loop.

Rounds 1–4 (5, 6, 7): Tr/dc 21 (25, 33, 37).

Round 5 (6, 7, 8): Tr/dc 13 (15, 20, 24).

Row 6 (7, 8, 9): *Turn, tr/dc 13 (15, 20, 24)*
*repeat 2 (3, 5, 5) times.

Fold hat so that the side of the rows touches the open area in the rounds. At the end of the last row, sl st rows to the rounds 2 (3, 4, 4) sts from where rows come out of rounds.

Sl st 4 (6, 7, 11), then sl st to connect rounds to end of opposite side of rows, tie off.

Dc/sc around the mouth opening with red yarn.

SHARK FIN

With hat colour ch 10.

Turn after each row.

Row 1: Sl st, dc/sc 1, tr/dc 4, dc/sc 1, sl st.

Row 2: Sl st, dc/sc 1, tr/dc 3, dc/sc 1, sl st.

Row 3: Sl st, dc/sc 1, tr/dc 2, dc/sc 1, sl st.

Row 4: Sl st, dc/sc 1, tr/dc 1, dc/sc 1, sl st.

Row 5: Sl st, tr/dc 1, dc/sc 1, sl st 4.

Row 6: Sl st 3, tr/dc 1, sl st 4. Tie off.

SHARK EYES

With black yarn, ch 3 and join in ring.

Dc/sc 4 in ring and tie off.

With white yarn dc/sc around ring and tie off.

Make 2.

SHARK TEETH

Ch 26.

Sl st, dc/sc 1, tr/dc 1, dc/sc 1, sl st, *repeat four more times across row, turn, sl st, tr/dc 1, *sl st 4, tr/dc 1*, *repeat twice more, sl st 2, tie off.

Make 2.

Use a needle and thread to sew on the eyes, fin and rows of teeth inside upper and lower sides of mouth opening.

Dogzilla Hat

Watch out metropolis...dogzilla is on the loose! This scaly hat can be paired with the dogzilla sweater for a fun and cosy costume.

Skill level: Intermediate

Materials
Crochet hook size: 10 mm (P, 000) for the hat and 6 mm (J/10, 4) for the decoration
Yarn: Super bulky (6)
    Extra small, 18 m(20 yd)
    Small, 23 m (25 yd)
    Medium, 27.5 m (30 yd)
    Large, 32 m (35 yd)

Colour B: for trim and scales: medium-weight (4), 2–3 m (yd)
Sewing needle and thread

Gauge 10 sts = 10 cm (4 in)
1 row tr/dc = (approximately) 2 cm (¾ in) high

EXTRA SMALL HAT

Leaving 15 cm (6 in) of yarn end for the hat tie, ch 17.

Row 1: Tr/dc in 4th ch from hook and tr/dc 15 across row, ch 3 and turn (first ch 3 counts as stitch for 16 total tr/dc).

Continue to turn after each row unless stated otherwise.

Row 2: Tr/dc 15 across row (16 total tr/dc).

Row 3: Sl st, tr/dc 13, sl st.

Row 4: Sl st, tr/dc 12, sl st.

Row 5: Sl st, ch 7, sk 3 and sl in fourth st (earhole), tr/dc 3 between ears, ch 7, sk 3 and sl in fourth st (other earhole), sl st.

Row 6: Sl st, dc/sc 2, sk 1, dc/sc 1, sk 1, dc/sc 2, tr/dc 3, dc/sc 2, dc/sc 2, sk 1, dc/sc 1, sk 1, dc/sc 2, sl st.

Row 7: Dc/sc 13, sl st 4 (1 in last sl st and sl st 3 down side of hat).

Row 8: Sl st 4 (back up side of hat), dc/sc 15, sl st 3 down opposite side of hat.

Tie off, leaving 15 cm (6 in) of yarn for hat tie.

SMALL HAT

Leaving 18 cm (7 in) of yarn end for string tie, ch 20.

Row 1: Tr/dc in fourth ch from hook and tr/dc 18 across row, ch 3 and turn (first ch 3 counts as stitch for 19 total tr/dc).

Continue to turn after each row unless stated otherwise.

Row 2: Tr/dc 18 across row (19 total tr/dc).

Row 3: Sl st, tr/dc 16, sl st.

Row 4: Sl st, tr/dc 15, sl st.

Row 5: Sl st, ch 8, sk 4 and sl in fifth st (earhole), tr/dc 4 between ears, ch 8, sk 4 and sl in fifth st (other earhole), sl st.

Row 6: Sl st, dc/sc 2, sk 1, dc/sc 2, sk 1, dc/sc 2, tr/dc 4, dc/sc 2, sk 1, dc/sc 2, sk 1, dc/sc 2, sl st.

Row 7: Dc/sc 16, sl st 6 (1 in last sl st and 5 sl st down side of hat).

Row 8: Sl st 5 (back up side of hat), dc/sc 18, sl st 3 down opposite side of hat.

Tie off, leaving 18 cm (7 in) of yarn for hat tie.

MEDIUM HAT

Leaving 18 cm (7 in) yarn on end for hat tie, ch 23.

Row 1: Tr/dc in fourth ch from hook and tr/dc 21 across row, ch 3 and turn (first ch 3 counts as stitch for 22 total tr/dc).

Continue to turn after each row unless stated otherwise.

Row 2: Tr/dc 21 across row (22 total tr/dc).

Row 3: Sl st, tr/dc 19, sl st.

Row 4: Sl st, tr/dc 18, sl st.

Row 5: Sl st, tr/dc 1, ch 8, sk 4 and sl st in fifth st (earhole), tr/dc 5 between ears, ch 8, sk 4 and sl st in fifth st (other earhole), tr/dc 1, sl st.

Row 6: Sl st, dc/sc 2, sk 1, dc/sc 2, sk 1, dc/sc 2, tr/dc 4, dc/sc 2, sk 1, dc/sc 2, sk 1, dc/sc 3, sl st.

Row 7: Dc/sc 17, sl st 6 (1 in last sl st and sl st 5 down side of hat).

Row 8: Sl st 5 (back up side of hat), dc/sc 19, sl st 3 down opposite side of hat.

Tie off, leaving 18 cm (7 in) for hat tie.

LARGE HAT

Leaving 20 cm (8 in) yarn on end for hat tie, ch 25.

Row 1: Tr/dc in fourth ch from hook and tr/dc 24 across row, ch 3 and turn (first ch 3 counts as stitch for 25 total tr/dc).

Continue to turn after each row unless stated otherwise.

Row 2: Tr/dc 24 across row (25 total tr/dc).

Row 3: Sl st, tr/dc 22, sl st.

Row 4: Sl st, tr/dc 21, sl st.

Row 5: Sl st, tr/dc 1, ch 9, sk 5 and sl st in sixth st (earhole), tr/dc 5 between ears, ch 9, sk 5 and sl st in sixth st (other earhole), tr/dc 1, sl st.

Row 6: Sl st, dc/sc 2, sk 1, dc/sc 3, sk 1, dc/sc 2, tr/dc 5, dc/sc 2, sk 1, dc/sc 3, sk 1, dc/sc 3, sl st.

Row 7: Dc/sc 19, sl st 6 (1 in last sl st and sl st 5 down side of hat).

Row 8: Sl st 5 (back up side of hat), dc/sc 21, sl st 3 down opposite side of hat.

Tie off, leaving 20 cm (8 in) for string tie.

HAT TRIM

Start in either corner of the hat (by string tie) and dc/sc around entire edge of hat one time for border. Tie off and weave in ends.

SCALES

Ch 7.

Sl st, dc/sc 2, tr/dc, dc/sc 2, sl st.

Sl st, dc/sc 2, tr/dc 2 in same st, dc/sc 2, sl st.

Sl st, dc/sc 2, tr/dc, dc/sc 2, sl st 2, tie off.

Make 3.

Weave in scale yarn ends, then sew scales down centre of hat with needle and thread.

The Great Pumpkin Dog Hat

This adorable hat will blend right in to the pumpkin patch. The hood buttons at the neck and is topped off with a stem, curly vine and leaves.

Skill level: Intermediate

Materials
Crochet hook size: 10 mm (P, 000) for the hat and 6 mm (J/10, 4) for the decoration
Yarn colour A: Super bulky (6)
Extra small, 27.5 m (30 yd)
Small, 41.25 m (45 yd)
Medium, 45.75 m (50 yd)
Large, 50.25 m (55 yd)

Colour B: medium-weight (4), for trim, leaves and vine, 12 yd (11 m)
Colour C: medium-weight (4), for stem, 5 yd (4.5 m)
2 buttons, each 25 mm (1 in) diameter
Sewing needle and thread

Gauge 10 sts = 10 cm (4 in)
1 row tr/dc = approximately 2 cm (¾ in) high

Note When working in rows, turn after each row unless stated otherwise.

EXTRA SMALL

Ch 22.

Note unless stated otherwise, start in second st from hook for sl st at beginning of row.

Row 1–2: Tr/dc 18 (total tr/dc 19 including first ch 3 from end of ch).

Row 3: Sl st, tr/dc 12 across then sl st leaving 4 on end.

Row 4: Sl st, tr/dc 11, sl st.

Row 5: Sl st, tr/dc 10, sl st.

Row 6: Sl st, tr/dc 9, sl st.

Row 7: Sl st, tr/dc 8, sl st.

Row 8: Sl st, tr/dc 7, sl st.

Row 9: Sl st 8 and tie off.

SMALL

Ch 27.

Row 1–3: Tr/dc 23 (total tr/dc 24 including first ch 3).

Row 4: Sl st, tr/dc 16, sl st, leaving 5 for strap.

Row 5: Sl st, tr/dc 15, sl st.

Row 6: Sl st, tr/dc 14, sl st.

Row 7: Sl st, tr/dc 13, sl st.

Row 8: Sl st, tr/dc 12, sl st.

Row 9: Sl st, tr/dc 11, sl st.

Row 10: Sl st 12 and tie off.

MEDIUM

Ch 30.

Row 1–3: Tr/dc 27 (total tr/dc 28 including first ch 3).

Row 4: Sl st, tr/dc 19, sl st, leaving 5 for strap.

Row 5: Sl st, tr/dc 18, sl st.

Row 6: Sl st, tr/dc 17, sl st.

Row 7: Sl st, tr/dc 16, sl st.

Row 8: Sl st, tr/dc 15, sl st.

Row 9: Sl st, tr/dc 14, sl st.

Row 10: Sl st 15 and tie off.

LARGE

Ch 33.

Row 1-3: Tr/dc 29 (total tr/dc 30 including first ch 3).

Row 4: Sl st, tr/dc 22, sl st, leaving 5 for strap.

Row 5: Sl st, tr/dc 21, sl st.

Row 6: Sl st, tr/dc 20, sl st.

Row 7: Sl st, tr/dc 19, sl st.

Row 8: Sl st, tr/dc 18, sl st.

Row 9: Sl st, tr/dc 17, sl st.

Row 10: Sl st, tr/dc 16, sl st.

Row 11: Sl st 17 and tie off.

TRIM

Using hook size 6 mm (J/10, 4) and medium weight yarn (4), dc/sc around hat to create trim.

Finishing

Sew two buttons to hat on opposite side to strap and use the open weave of the crochet as buttonholes. Place one button at the base of the hat 1.5 cm (½ in) from back edge and a second one about 5 cm (2 in) above it, also 1.5 cm (½ in) from back edge of hat.

STEM

Ch 3 and join in circle.

Dc/sc 8 rows and tie off.

VINE

Ch 12.

Sl st down chain and tie off.

LEAVES

Ch 6.

Sl st in third loop from hook to form a ring with stem.

Htrc/hdc 3, ch 3, sl st, htrc/hdc 4, sl st 2 down stem. Tie off ends.

Frog Hat

Bundle up your pet in this snuggly and fun hood-style frog hat. It is sure to make passers-by smile on the walk.

Skill level: Intermediate

Materials

Crochet hook size: 9 mm (N/14, 00) and
    6 mm (J/10, 4)
Yarn: Super bulky (6) 46 m (50 yd)
    Medium-weight (4) in pink, black and
    white, 4.5 m (5 yd) of each
Sewing needle and thread

Gauge 10 sts = 10 cm (4 in)
1 row tr/dc = approximately
    2 cm (¾ in) high

HAT BASE

USing the 9 mm crochet hook, ch 24 (28, 36, 40) and join in a loop.

Rounds 1–4 (5, 6, 7): Tr/dc 21 (25, 33, 37).

Round 5 (6, 7, 8): Tr/dc 13 (15, 20, 24).

Row 6 (7, 8, 9): *Turn, tr/dc 13 (15, 20, 24)* repeat 2 (3, 5, 5) times.

Fold hat so that the side of the rows touches the open area in the rounds. At the end of the last row, sl st rows to the rounds 2 (3, 4, 4) sts from where rows come out of rounds.

Sl st 4 (6, 7, 11), then sl st to connect rounds to end of opposite side of rows, tie off.

FROG EYES OUTER

Using 9 mm (N/14, 00) hook size and super bulky (6) yarn, ch 3 and join in loop.

Round 1: Dc/sc 5 in loop and sl st to join, ch 1.

Round 2: Dc/sc, dc/sc 2 in next st, dc/sc, dc/sc 2 in next st, dc/sc, dc/sc 2 in next st (total dc/sc 9).

Round 3: Dc/sc 8 and do not join, tie off.

Make 2.

FROG EYES INNER

Using 6 mm (J/10, 4) crochet hook and medium-weight black yarn, ch 3 and join in loop.

Round 1: Dc/sc 5 in loop and sl st to join, ch 1.

Round 2: Dc/sc, dc/sc 2 in next st, dc/sc, dc/sc 2 in next st, dc/sc, dc/sc 2 in next st (9 total dc/sc) tie off.

Round 3: Join white yarn and ch 1, dc/sc 9 around and join.

Round 4: Dc/sc, dc/sc 2 in next st, dc/sc, dc/sc 2 in next st, dc/sc, dc/sc 2, dc/sc, dc/sc 2 in next st total dc/sc (12).

Tie off.

FROG TONGUE

Using 6 mm (J/10, 4) crochet hook and medium-weight yarn in red, ch 3 and join in a loop.

Dc/sc 5 in loop.

Dc/sc 2, dc/sc 2 in next st, dc/sc, dc/sc 2 in next st, sl st to join.

Dc/sc 2, dc/sc 2 in next st, dc/sc, dc/sc 2 in next st, do not join, tie off.

Join pink yarn dc/sc 10 and tie off.

With a needle and thread, sew the eye inners to eye outers, and then sew eyes to top of hat about 2.5 cm (1 in) from face opening. Sew tongue to bottom of mouth opening.

Accessories

Crocheted Flower Corsage

A delicate burst of colour is just the thing to brighten up your dog's collar. These collar corsages are an easy and comfortable way to dress up your pet's appearance for a special occasion or a day on the town.

Skill level: Intermediate

Materials
Crochet hook sizes: 9 mm (N, 00) and 6 mm (J/10, 4)
Yarn: super bulky (6):4 m (4 yd)
    Medium-weight (4) cotton, acrylic or
    wool yarn 4.75 m (5 yd)
Needle and thread
Elastic, 4 cm (1½ in)
Fabric glue
Button: 1.5 cm (½ in)

FLOWER OUTER
With 9 mm (N/14, 00) hook and super-bulky weight yarn, ch 4 and join in ring.
Htr/hdc 5 in ring and sl st to join.
Ch 4 and sl st in next, repeat around circle to form petals.
Tie off and trim ends.

FLOWER INNER
Using 6 mm (J/10, 4) crochet hook and medium-weight yarn, ch 4.
Htr/hdc 5 in ring and sl st to join.
Ch 4 and sl st in next, repeat around circle to form petals.
Tie off and trim ends.
Sew flower inner to flower outer and sew leaf to the back on one side.
Sew the button to the flower centre.
Take 4 cm (1½ in) elastic and use fabric glue to create a loop.
Sew the loop to the back of the flower.

LEAF
Ch 6.
Sl st in third loop from hook to form a ring with stem.
Htc/hdc 3, ch 3, sl st, htc/hdc 4, sl st 2 down stem.
Tie off ends.

Granny Square Scarf

Granny squares are a classic crocheted motif and can be combined to create a variety of projects. Sew several squares together end to end and adjust to suit your pet's neck size. These basic squares are simple to master and once you get the hang of making them, you may not stop! Piecing together granny squares is an easy way to make cosy blankets and other projects for your pet dog.

Skill level: Intermediate

Materials
Crochet hook size: 6 mm (J/10, 4)
Yarn: Medium-weight (4)
Sewing needle and thread
1 button: 25 mm (1 in) diameter

Gauge is not critical for this project.

Sizes:
Extra small, 6 squares, 51 cm/20 in long
Small,　　 7 squares, 58 cm/23 in long
Medium,　 8 squares, 66 cm/26 in long
Large,　　 10 squares, 76 cm/30 in long

SQUARE
Ch 5 and join in a loop.
Ch 3 (this is your first tr/dc) and tr/dc 2 in loop,
Ch 2 and tr/dc 3 in loop. Repeat twice more to create the four corners of the starter square.
Tie off.
Round 1: Join next yarn colour in corner of square where you tied off. Ch 3, tr/dc 3, ch 2, tr/dc 3 in corner.
Ch 1 and tr/dc 3, ch 2, tr/dc 3 in next corner. Repeat in next two corners.
Join with sl st in third chain on first corner.
Tie off.
Round 2: Join next yarn of yarn in ch 1 space (side of square inbetween the corners), ch 3 and tr/dc 2 in ch 1.

*Ch 1 and tr/dc 3, ch 2, tr/dc 3 in corner.
Ch 1 and tr/dc 3 in next ch 1 space*. Repeat around square and join with sl st in ch 3 of your first stitch
Tie off.

Sew the squares end to end using a needle and thread. Attach the button to the left side of the scarf and use the open weave of the crochet as a buttonhole. Our button is attached to the bottom of the second square on the left side of the scarf, but try the scarf on your pet first to work out the best location for an exact fit around the neck.

The Scholar

When your dog stares off into the distance, you know he is contemplating the universe and all its mysteries. This neck warmer keeps your learned pooch cosy by protecting the neck and face from wind and rain. A small ruffle around the edge lends a sophisticated flair.

Skill level: Easy

Materials
Crochet hook size: 10 mm (P, 000)
Yarn: Super bulky (6)
    Extra small, 32 m (36 yd)
    Small, 39 m (43 yd)
    Medium, 50 m (55 yd)
    Large, 55 m (60 yd)

Gauge:10 sts = 10 cm (4 in)
1 row tr/dc = (approximately) 2 cm (¾ in) high

Neck circumference size
Extra small, 24 cm (9½ in)
Small,   30 cm (12 in)
Medium,   39.5 cm (15½ in)
Large,   46 cm (18 in)

Instructions are written for the Extra small size with (Small, Medium, Large) presented in brackets.

Ch 23 (28, 35, 42) and create a ring.
Work 5 rows tr/dc.
On the next row, tr/dc around but do not join ring, turn and tr/dc 4 more rows and do not join.
Ch 3, sl st, *ch 2, sl st* and repeat * around top of collar, ch 3 and sl st in last stitch to create ruffled edge along top.

The Count

Muahaha... This distinguished black and scarlet collar is fitting for the noblest of pets, especially those with a penchant for the dark side. The chunky yarn stands up high around the neck so it's also a great way to keep your pet's face warm and toasty during the walk (or stalk).

Skill level: Intermediate

Crochet hook sizes: 10 mm (P, 000) for main body and 6 mm (J/10, 4) for the trim

Yarn colour A: Super bulky (6)
    Extra small, 27.5 m (30 yd)
    Small, 32 m (35 yd)
    Medium, 41.25 m (45 yd)
    Large, 45.75 m (50 yd)

Colour B: medium-weight (4)
    9–14 m (10–15 yd)

Button

Gauge 10 sts = 10 cm (4 in)
1 row tr/dc = approximately 2 cm (¾ in) high

Finished collar dimensions

Extra small,	24 cm (9½ in)
Small,	30.5 cm (12 in)
Medium,	39.5 cm (15½ in)
Large,	46 cm (18 in)

Instructions are written for the Extra Small size with (Small, Medium, Large) presented in brackets.

Ch 23 (28, 35, 42) and create a ring.
Work 4 rows tr/dc.
On the next row tr/dc around but do not join ring, turn and tr/dc 4 more rows and do not join.
Sl st down and around the V shape in the front of the collar and tie off.

Using 6 mm (J/10, 4) crochet hook and medium-weight red yarn, dc/sc around top edge.
Ch 3 and join in loop.
Htrc/hdc 4 in loop and join.
Tie off.
Sew circle to centre of collar and sew a fancy button into centre of the circle.

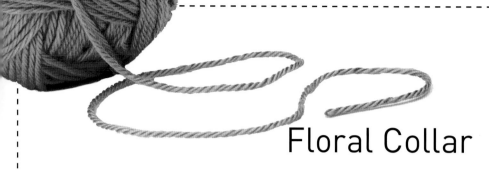

Floral Collar

A small bouquet of delicate flowers adorns this easy-to-create collar.
This comfy floral collar is a wonderful way to dress up a pet without them being
any the wiser. Create them in custom colours to include your furry pal in the
wedding party.

Skill level: Intermediate

Materials

Crochet hook sizes: 10 mm (P, 000), 9 mm
 (N/14, 00) and 6 mm (J/10, 4)
Yarn colour A super bulky (6):
  Extra small, 9 m (10 yd)
  Small, 13.75 m (15 yd)
  Medium, 18.25 m (20 yd)
  Large, 23 m (25 yd)
Colour B: Medium-weight (4) for the flower: 1 m (yd)
Colour C: Medium-weight (4) for the flower: 1 m (yd)
Colour D: Medium-weight (4) for the flower 1 m (yd)
Colour E: Medium-weight (4) for the leaf: 2 yd

Gauge 10 sts = 10 cm (4 in)
1 row tr/dc = approximately 2 cm (¾ in)
  high.
Gauge is not important for the flowers and leaves

Finished collar dimensions

Extra small,   24 cm (9½ in)
Small,   30 cm (12 in)
Medium,   39.5 cm (15½ in)
Large,   46 cm (18 in)

COLLAR BASE

With 10 mm (P, 000) crochet hook and yarn A
ch 23 (28, 35, 42) and join in a ring.
Work 2 rows tr/dc.
Work 1 row dc/sc.

FLOWER OUTER

With 9 mm (N/14, 00) crochet hook and yarn B
super bulky col B, ch 4 and join in ring.
Htc/hdc 5 in ring and join.
Ch 4 and sl st in next st, repeat around circle to
form petals.
Tie off and trim ends.

FLOWER INNER

With 6 mm (J/4) crochet hook and mediumweight
yarn C, ch 4.
Round 1: Htrc/hdcr 5 in ring and sl st to join, tie off.
Join in yarn D anywhere on ring.
Round 2: *Ch 4 and sl st in next st*, repeat around
circle to form petals.
Tie off and trim ends.

Sew flower inner to flower outer and sew leaf to the
back on one side.

LEAF

Ch 6 using yarn E.
Sl st in third loop from hook to form a ring with
stem.
Htrc/hdc 3, ch 3, sl st, htrc/hdc 4, sl st 2 down stem.
Tie off ends.

Jolly Holly Collar

Even your pup will get into the holiday spirit with this festive holly collar.
Sew small bells in the centre of the holly berries to give it a jingle – also a good
way to hear your dog snooping around the holiday feast!

Skill level: Intermediate

Materials
Crochet hook sizes: 10 mm (P, 000), 6 mm (J, 4)
Yarn colour A: super bulky (6)
    Extra small, 9 m (10 yd)
    Small:, 13.75 m (15 yd)
    Medium, 18.25 m (20 yd)
    Large, 23 m (25 yd)
Colour B: medium-weight (4) for berries, 7.5 m
    (8 yd)
Colour C: medium-weight (4) for leaves 7.5 m (8 yd)
3 small silver bells

Gauge 10 sts = 10 cm (4 in)
1 row tr/dc = approximately 2 cm (¾ in) high.
Gauge is not important for holly berries or leaves.

Finished collar dimensions
Extra small	24 cm (9½ in)
Small	30 cm (12 in)
Medium	39.5 cm (15½ in)
Large	46 cm (18 in)

COLLAR BASE
With 10 mm (P, 000) crochet hook and yarn A, ch 23
(28, 35, 42) and join in a ring.
Turn after each row, continue to join each round to
the next. Work 4 rounds tr/dc.
Tie off.

BERRIES
With 6 mm (J/10, 4) crochet hook and yarn B, ch 3
and join in ring.
Ch 1 and dc/sc 5 in ring and join.
Ch 1 and dc/sc 5, inc 1 and join.
Tie off. Make 3.

LEAVES
With 6 mm (J/10, 4) crochet hook and yarn C, ch 6.
Sl st in third loop from hook to form a ring
with stem.
Htrc/hdc 3, ch 3, sl st, htrc/hdc 4, sl st 2 down stem.
Skip over stem and start work around the outside of
the leaf, ch 3 and sl st in next st.
Ch 2 and sl st in next st.
Sl st 6 up around tip of leaf.
Ch 2 and sl st in next st.
Ch 3 and sl st in next st.
Sl st down leaf stem and tie off. Make 2.

Sew two leaves onto collar. Place three berries
on top of stems of holly leaves and sew into place.
Sew bells into the centre of the berries, if desired.

Note Bells can be tempting to pets, who may
mistake them for toys. As with all pet apparel,
it is best not to leave apparel on or near your pet
while unattended.

Leg Warmers

Leg warmers are not only a fashionable throwback to the '80s, they are also a comfy way to keep little legs warm and dry. These striped tubes are worked in the round and can be customised to fit your pet's leg height.

Skill level: Easy

Materials
Crochet hook size: 6.5 mm (K/10.5, 3)
Yarn: Medium-weight (4)

Gauge: 4 sts = 2.5 cm (1 in)

Suggested size:
    Extra small: 3 stripes, 9 cm (3½ in) long to fit
      9 cm (3½ in) leg circumference
    Small: 4 stripes, 13 cm (5 in) long to fit 10 cm
      (4 in) leg circumference
    Medium: 6 stripes, 19 cm (7½ in) long to fit 12 cm
      (4¾ in) leg circumference
    Large: 8 stripes, 25 cm (10 in) long to fit 14.5 cm
      (5¾ in) leg circumference

Note The circumference of the leg warmer should be slightly smaller than your pet's leg circumference so that they stay up. If you prefer to use elastic in the top of the warmers, add 2-3 stitches to your choice of size to achieve a looser fit.

Instructions are written for the Extra small size with (Small, Medium, Large) presented in brackets.

Ch 12 (14, 18, 22) and join in ring (or measure circumference of widest part of the top of your pet's leg and use this as your base chain).
Work 5 rows dc/sc in first yarn, tie off.
*Join next yarn with dc/sc and dc/sc 5 rows, tie off.
*Repeat until leg warmers are the right height for your pet. The leg warmers featured are four stripes (20 rows dc/sc).

Soft Sweaters

Button-neck Sweater

This chunky sweater fastens with a button at the neck for an adjustable fit that's just right. This style is a great fit for pets that prefer not to have a sweater go on over their head, and most dogs enjoy warm gear that goes on and off quickly without a fuss. The open chest allows for maximum comfort and ease of movement.

Skill level: Easy

Materials
Crochet hook size: 10 mm (P, 000)
Yarn: Super Bulky (6)
    Extra small, 78 m (85 yd)
    Small, 96 m (105 yd)
    Medium, 114 m (125 yd)
    Large, 133 m (145 yd)
Button: 4 cm (1½ in)
Sewing needle and thread

Gauge 10 sts = 10 cm (4 in)
1 row tr/dc = approximately 2 cm (¾ in) high.

Finished sweater dimensions

	Collar width	Chest	Length
X small	28 cm (11 in)	36 cm (14¼ in)	30.5cm (12 in)
Small	33 cm (13 in)	42 cm (16½ in)	37 cm (14½ in)
Medium	39 cm (15½ in)	49 cm (19 in)	44 cm (17¼ in)
Large	47 cm (18½ in)	59 cm (23 in)	53.5 cm (21 in)

Note This sweater will stretch 5–7.5 cm (2-3 in) for the smallest sizes and as much as 12.5 cm (5 in) for the larger sizes. It is designed to fit the small end of each size range. Crochet a smaller size if your pet is between sizes. Alternatively reduce or increase stitches in the base chain or chest to adjust the fit. The open weave will be used to button the sweater, making the neck very adjustable.

Instructions are written for the Extra small size with (Small, Medium, Large) presented in brackets.

COLLAR

Ch 26 (29, 35, 40).

Rows 1–3 (4, 5, 6): Tr/dc 3 (4, 5, 6) rows, ch 3 and turn after each row (23, 26, 32, 37).

Rows: 4 (5, 6, 7) Dc/sc 1 (1, 0, 0), turn.

NECK

Row 5 (6, 6, 7): in second st from hook, sl st 5 (5, 6,8), ch 2 and do not turn, tr/dc 12 (15, 17, 20) across, ch 1 and turn (Large: ch 3 and turn).

Row 6 (7, 7, 8): Dc/sc 12 (15, 17, 20).

CHEST AND BELLY

Ch 18 (18, 22, 28) and connect to opposite side with sl st for chest.

Ch 3 and turn.

Note When working tr/dc in round for chest, ch 3 and turn after each row unless stated otherwise.

Rounds 1–7 (8, 9, 14): Tr/dc 7 (8, 9, 14) rows around chest.

After completing last row, do not ch 3.

RUMP

Row 1: Sl st 2 (2, 2, 3) towards underside of sweater, *ch 3 and turn, tr/dc 16 (18, 21, 26)*.

Rows 2–5 (6, 7): *Repeat for 4 (5, 6, 7) additional rows.

Last row: Sl st down side of sweater and all the way around underside and opposite side, tie off.

Note: Dogs vary widely in proportion, so if your dog is longer just add additional rows of tr/dc at the end of this pattern and then sl st around and tie off.

Weave in ends and sew button to left side of collar approximately 2 cm (¾ in) from edge. Use the open weave of the crochet as a buttonhole.

High Collar Sweater with Stripe

The high collar on this sweater folds up or down to protect ears from the damp and drizzle. The chest piece provides extra warmth through the core and a sharp looking stripe adds classic style.

Skill level: Intermediate

Crochet hook size: 10 mm (P, 000) and
   6 mm (J/10, 4)
Yarn colour A: Super bulky (6)
   Extra small, 64 m (70 yd)
   Small, 87 m (95 yd)
   Medium, 116 m (125 yd)
   Large ,133 m (145 yd)
Colour B: for stripe and accent
   Extra small, 23 m (25 yd)
   Small, 23 m (25 yd)
   Medium, 27 m (30 yd)
   Large, 37 m (40 yd)

Gauge 10 sts = 10 cm (4 in).
1 row tr/dc = approximately 2 cm (¾ in)
   high

Finished sweater dimensions

	Collar width	Chest	Length
X small	28 cm (11 in)	36 cm (14¼ in)	30.5cm (12 in)
Small	33 cm (13 in)	42 cm (16½ in)	37 cm (14½ in)
Medium	39 cm (15½ in)	49 cm (19 in)	44 cm (17¼ in)
Large	47 cm (18½ in)	59 cm (23 in)	53.5 cm (21 in)

Instructions are written for the Extra small size with (Small, Medium, Large) presented in brackets. Ch 24 (26, 30, 34) and join in ring for neck.

Round 1: Ch 3 and begin tr/dc in third loop from hook, *tr/dc 21 (23, 27, 31) around neck and sl st to join, ch 3*.

Rounds 2–3 (–3, –3, –4): *Repeat 2 (2, 2, 3) times, do not ch 3 on round 3 (3, 3, 4).

Round 4 (4, 4, 5): Turn, sl st 5 (7, 8, 9) begin sl st in second st from hook.

Round 5 (5, 5, 6): Ch 3 and tr/dc around leaving 6 (7, 8, 9) on opposite side.

Round 6 (6, 6, 7): Ch 1 and turn, dc/sc 1 row.

Round 7 (7, 7, 8): Ch 16 (20, 23, 25) and join to opposite side for chest, ch 3 and turn.

Note when working dc in round in chest ch 3 and turn after each row tr/dc unless stated otherwise.

Rounds 8 (8–9, 8–9, 9–10): tr/dc 1 (2, 2, 2) rows and tie off.

Round 9 (10, 10, 11): join colour B with sl st starting in centre of bottom of chest and tr/dc around, sl st to join.

Rounds 10–12 (11–15, 11–15, 12–17): Tr/dc 4 (6, 6, 7) rows and tie off.

Round: 13 (16, 16, 18): Join yarn A with sl st 6 (7, 8, 9) stitches from where you tied off yarn B (on each side of sl st).

Row 1: Ch 3 and tr/dc across, leaving 6 (7, 8, 9) on opposite side, ch 3 and turn.

Note Ch 3 and turn at end of the following tr/dc rows, except for last row 5 (6, 7, 8).

Rows 2–5 (–6, –7, –8): Tr/dc 4 (5, 6, 7) additional rows, ch 2 and turn at end of last row.

Row 6 (7, 8, 9): Row dc/sc last row.

Row 7 (8, 9, 10): Sl st down side and all the way around end of sweater and tie off.

CHEST PIECE

Count 6 (7, 8, 9) stitches from where front leg area meets chest.

Row 1: Dc/sc across, leaving 6 (7, 8, 9) stitches on opposite side.

Rows 2–5: Work 4 rows dc/sc.

Row 6: Dc/sc and dec 1 (sk) in middle of row.

Rows 7–8: Work 2 additional rows dc/sc.

Tie off leaving 25 cm/10 in of yarn.

Use excess yarn and 6 mm (J/10, 4) crochet hook to weave the chest piece end into centre of the neck portion of sweater. The yarn tail from beginning of the collar indicates where the centre of the collar is. Align the centre of the chest piece with the centre of the collar. Fold sweater in half lengthwise to check that the legholes are the same size.

COLLAR

Starting in centre of neck, *sl st, tr/dc around neck and sl st in last stitch.

Turn and sl st, tr/dc around neck and sl st in last stitch, turn*.

Repeat from * to * for 4 (5, 5, 6) more rows.

With yarn B, sl st around neck of collar and tie off.

Weave in all ends on the wrong side.

Winter Coat

This sweater drapes over your dog's back and also covers the top of the chest and legs. A chest piece connects the sweater underneath the belly and keeps it in place. The button neck uses the open weave of the sweater as buttonholes, making it very adjustable.

Skill level Beginner

Materials
Crochet hook size: 10 mm
  (P, 000)
Yarn A: super bulky (6)
  Extra small, 78 m (85 yd)
  Small, 96 m (105 yd)
  Medium, 123 m (135 yd)
  Large, 142 m/155 yd
Yarn B: Super bulky (6):
  Extra small, 32 m (35 yd)
  Small, 41 m (45 yd)
  Medium, 46 m (50 yd)
  Large, 55 m (60 yd)

Gauge 10 sts = 10 cm (4 in)
1 row tr/dc = approximately
  2 cm (¾ in) high.

Finished sweater dimensions

	Collar Width	Back Width	Chest	Length
XSmall	33 cm (16 in)	36 cm (14 in)	36 cm (14¼ in)	30.5 cm (12 in)
Small	41 cm (19 in)	42 cm (16½ in)	42 cm (16½ in)	37 cm (14½ in)
Medium	46 cm (21 in)	47 cm (18½ in)	49 cm (20 in)	44 cm (17¼ in)
Large	52 cm (24 in)	53 cm (21 in)	59 cm (24 in)	53.5 cm (21 in)

Note The collar will overlap 5–7.5 cm (2–3 in) at neck to fasten button. Smaller sweaters will stretch about 2.5–5 cm (1–2 in) with wear. Medium and Large will stretch up to 9 cm (3½ in) with wear. Add additional stitches to base chain to make the neck larger. Adding 2 st to base chain will add 2.5 cm (1 in) to neck and also add an additional 2.5 cm (1 in) to width of back. Add 1 sl st in row 5 for additional 2 sts added in base chain to keep back same size.

SWEATER BASE

Ch 25 (34, 36, 40).

Row 1: Turn and tr/dc in fourth ch from hook, tr/dc 22 (31, 33, 37) across row, ch 3 and turn at end of row (total tr/dc 23 (32, 34, 38)).

Rows 2–4: *Tr/dc across row, ch 3 and turn* repeat twice (total rows tr/dc 3).

Ch 2 and turn at end of fourth row.

Row 5: Dc/sc 1 row, turn and sl st 4 (5, 5, 6) (beginning sl st in second st from hook).

Row 6: Ch 3 and tr/dc 13 (21, 22, 25) across leaving 5 (6, 6, 7) stitches on opposite side, ch 3 and turn.

Rows 7–18 (7–20, 7–22, 7–24): Tr/dc 10 (12, 14, 16) rows and tie off.

BORDER

With yarn B join anywhere on outside of sweater base and *ch 3, then tr/dc all the way around sweater, turn*. Repeat twice more for 3 rows tr/dc around edge of sweater.

CHEST PIECE

Leaving 20 cm (8 in) of yarn, ch 16 (20, 23, 25).

Tr/dc 5 (7, 7, 8) rows.

Tie off leaving 25 cm (10 in) of yarn.

Attach chest piece 2.5 cm (1 in) below T shape in sweater on the underside. Sew in excess yarn.

Weave in ends and sew buttons to left-hand side of the collar, lined up vertically approximately 2.5 cm (1 in) from edge. Use the open weave of the crochet as buttonholes for an adjustable fit.

Dogzilla Sweater

Keep your furry monster of any size warm and comfy with this cloak-style sweater. Combine this with the dogzilla hat for a costume that's adorable and functional.

Skill level: Intermediate

Materials

Crochet hook sizes: 10 mm (P, 000) and 6mm (J/10, 44) for the scales

Yarn colour A: super bulky (6)
Extra small, 69 m (75 yd)
Small, 87 m (95 yd)
Medium, 110 m (120 yd)
Large, 133 m (145 yd)

Yarn B: medium weight:
Extra small, 28 m (30 yd)
Small, 37 m (40 yd)
Medium, 44 m (48 yd)
Large, 49 m (54 yd)

Gauge 10 sts = 10 cm (4 in)
1 row tr/dc = approximately 2 cm (¾ in) high

Finished sweater dimensions

	Collar width	Back width	Chest	Length
XSmall	33 cm (13 in)	28 cm (11 in)	36 cm (14¼ in)	30.5 cm (11 in)
Small	41 cm (16 in)	34 cm (13½ in)	42 cm (16½ in)	37 cm (13 in)
Medium	46 cm (18 in)	40 cm (15½ in)	51 cm (20 in)	44 cm (17 in)
Large	52 cm (20½ in)	46 cm (18 in)	61 cm (24 in)	51 cm (20 in)

Note The collar will overlap 5–7.5 cm (2-3 in) at neck to fasten button. Smaller sweaters will stretch about 2.5–5 cm (1–2 in) with wear, Medium and Large will stretch up to 9 cm (3½ in) with wear. Add additional stitches to the base chain to make the neck larger. Adding 2 st to base chain will add 2.5 cm (1 in) to neck and to width of back. Add 1 sl st in row 5 per additional 2 sts added in base chain to keep back same size.

Instructions are written for the Extra small size with (Small, Medium, Large) presented in brackets.

SWEATER BASE

Ch 21 (30, 32, 36).

Row 1: Turn and tr/dc in fourth ch from hook, tr/dc 18 (27, 29, 33) across row, ch 3 and turn at end of row (total tr/dc 1 9 (28, 30:, 34]).

Rows 2–4: *Tr/dc across row, ch 3 and turn* repeat twice (total rows tr/dc 3).
Ch 2 and turn at end of fourth row.

Row 5: Dc/sc 1 row, turn and sl st 3 (5, 5, 6) (begin sl st in second st from hook).

Row 6: Ch 3 and tr/dc 11 (16, 18, 20) across leaving 4 (6, 6, 7) stitches on opposite side, ch 3 and turn.

Rows 7–18 (7–20, 7–22, 7–24): Tr/dc 12 (14, 16, 18) rows and tie off.

SWEATER BORDER

With yarn B join anywhere on outside of sweater base and *ch 3, then tr/dc all the way around sweater, turn*. Repeat once more for 2 rows tr/dc around edge of sweater.

CHEST PIECE

Leaving 20 cm (8 in) of yarn, ch 16 (20, 23, 25).
Tr/dc 5 (7, 7, 8) rows.
Tie off leaving 25 cm (10 in) of yarn.
Attach chest piece 2.5 cm (1 in) below T-shape in sweater on the underside.

SCALES

Ch 7.
Sl st, dc/sc 2, tr/dc, dc/sc 2, sl st.
Sl st, dc/sc 2, tr/dc 2 in same st, dc/sc 2, sl st.
Sl st, dc/sc 2, tr/dc, dc/sc 2, sl st 2, tie off.
Make 5–7.

Weave in scale ends, then sew scales down spine of sweater with needle and thread. Sew buttons vertically to left-hand side of collar, approximately 2.5 cm (1 in) from edge.

Capelet

This stylish cape is made using herringbone stitch, which gives a unique texture. A small ruffled edge adorns the top and bottom and is attached with a button at the neck.

Skill level: Intermediate

Crochet hook size: 6.5 mm (K,3)
Yarn: Medium-weight
    Extra small, 41 m (45 yd)
    Small, 55 m (60 yd)
    Medium, 69 m (75 yd)
    Large, 87 m (95 yd)

Gauge 16 sts = 10 cm (4 in)

Finished capelet dimensions

	Neck	Chest/strap	Bottom width
XSmall	19 cm (7½ in)	28 cm (11 in)	29 cm (11½ in)
Small	28 cm (11 in)	37 cm (14½ in)	38 cm (15 in)
Medium	32 cm (12½ in)	41 cm (16 in)	42 cm (16½ in)
Large	42 cm (16½ in)	51 cm (20 in)	52 cm (20½ in)

SPECIAL STITCHES:

Htrc/Hdc: Herringbone Treble Crochet/
   Herringbone Double Crochet
Yo: Insert hook into st, yo, pull through (3 loops on
   hook), pull through first loop on hook (without
   another yo), then yo and draw through 2 rem
   loops on hook.

Instructions are written for the Extra small size
with Small, Medium, Large presented in brackets.

Ch 28 (35, 42, 52) and do not join.
Row 1: *Tr/dc around row, ch 3 and turn*.
Row 2: *Repeat for one more row.
Row 3: Tr/dc and increase twice in row (tr/dc 2
stitches in 1 st).
Ch 9 and turn.
Tr/dc across row, ch 3 and turn.
Tr/dc 32 (39, 46, 56), ch 4 and leave 2 for button hole,
1 tr/dc.
Tr/dc across, ch 3 and turn.
Tr/dc 27 (34, 41, 51), ch 3 and turn.
Note: Ch 3 and turn after each row of htrc/hdc.
Htrc/hdc 4 rows.
Htrc/hdc increase twice on row 5.

EXTRA SMALL AND SMALL SIZE

Ch 3, sl st and repeat* across row for ruffle
around bottom.
Sl st up side and around button strap.
Ch 2, sl st and repeat * across row for ruffle
around top.
Sl st down opposite side and tie off.

MEDIUM (LARGE) SIZE

Herringbone htrc/hdc 4 (6) additional rows.
Ch 3, sl st and repeat* across row for ruffle
around bottom.
Sl st up side and around button strap.
Ch 2, sl st and repeat * across row for ruffle
around top.
Sl st down opposite side and tie off.

Sew button on cape on opposite side of strap.

Ruffled-neck Sweater

The fancy edging on the neck of this sweater is sure to suit the stateliest of dogs. The high neck will also help protect your pal's furry face from the elements.

Skill level: Intermediate

Materials
Crochet hook size: 10 mm (P, 000)
Yarn: Super bulky (6)
    Extra small, 78 m/85 yd
    Small, 96 m/105 yd
    Medium, 14 m/125 yd
    Large, 137 m/150 yd

Gauge 10 sts = 10 cm (4 in)
    1 row tr/dc = approximately
      2 cm (¾ in) high

Finished sweater dimensions

	Collar width	Chest	Length
XSmall	28 cm (11 in)	36 cm (14¼ in)	30.5 cm (12 in)
Small	33 cm (13 in)	42 cm (16½ in)	37 cm (14½ in)
Medium	39 cm (15½ in)	51 cm (20 in)	44 cm (17½ in)
Large	47 cm (18½ in)	61 cm (24 in)	53.5 cm (21 in)

Instructions are written for the Extra small size with Small, Medium, Large presented in brackets.

Ch 24 (26, 30, 34) and join in a ring.
Round 2: Ch 3 and begin tr/dc in fourth loop from hook, tr/dc around ring.
Rounds 3–4 (4, 4, 5): Complete 2 (2, 2, 3) additional rows of tr/dc.
Round 5 (5, 5, 6): Sl 5 (7, 8, 9), ch 3 and tr/dc around leaving (7, 8, 9) on opposite side.
Round 6 (6, 6, 7): Ch 1 and turn, dc/sc 1 row across, at end of row ch 16 (20, 23, 25) and join to opposite side for chest.
Round 7 (7, 7, 8): *Ch 3 and turn, tr/dc around and sl to join*.
Rounds 8–14 (14, 14, 15): *Repeat for 7 (10, 11, 12) rows.

Row 1 (sweater rump): Ch 3 and tr/dc across top of sweater, fold sweater in half lengthwise, and end rump leaving 6 (7, 8, 9) on opposite side so two halves of rump match.
Rows 2–6 (7, 8, 10): Tr/dc 5 (6, 7, 9) more rows.
Row 7 (8, 9, 11): Dc/sc last row, sl down side and all the way around end of sweater, tie off.

RUFFLED COLLAR
Row 1: Starting in middle of front of neck, dc around neck and do not join, ch 3 and turn.
Rows 2–5 (6, 6, 7): Tr/dc 4 (5, 5, 6) additional rows.
Row 6 (7, 7, 8): Ch 3, sl st in next st, *ch 2 and sl st in next stitch* and *repeat around neck, ch 3 and sl st in last stitch.
Tie off.

Turtleneck Sweater

This sweater has good coverage through the neck, chest and rump to keep your dog warm. The round doily appliqué can be placed on either side of the neck or rump, or create several in a variety of colours for a fun and funky look.

Skill level: Intermediate

Materials
Crochet hook size: 9 mm (N/14, 00) for sweater and 6.5 mm (K/10.5, 3) for appliqué
Yarn: Bulky (5)
    Extra small, 96 m, (105 yd)
    Small, 114 m, (125 yd)
    Medium, 133 m, (145 yd)
    Large, 160 m, (175 yd)
Sewing needle and thread

Gauge: 12 sts = 10 cm (4 in)

Finished sweater dimensions

	Collar width	Chest	Length
XSmall	28 cm (11 in)	36 cm (14¼ in)	30 cm (12 in)
Small	33 cm (13 in)	42 cm (16½ in)	37 cm (14½ in)
Medium	39 cm (15½ in)	51 cm (20 in)	44 cm (17½ in)
Large	47 cm (18½ in)	61 cm (24 in)	53.5 cm (21 in)

Instructions are written for the Extra small size with Small, Medium, Large presented in brackets.

Ch 26 (28, 32, 36) and join in ring.
Round 1–5 (6, 7, 9): Ch 3 and turn, dc 5 (6, 7, 9) rows.
Round 6 (7, 8, 10): Sl st 6 (7, 8, 9), ch 3, tr/dc across leaving 6 (7, 8, 9) on opposite side.
Round 7 (8, 9, 11): Ch 2 and turn, dc/sc across row, ch 17 (20, 25, 32) for chest and join with sl st on opposite side.
Round 8–15 (9-18, 10-21, 12-25): *Ch 3 and turn, tr/dc around ring, sl st to join each round*.
*Repeat for 7 (9, 11, 12) more rounds, do not ch 3 at end of last round and do not turn.
Round 9 (9, 11, 13): Sl st 3 and tr/dc across top portion of sweater, stopping 3 sts past front leg hole on opposite side – this forms the rump portion of the sweater.

Fold sweater in half lengthwise to make sure both sides of the rump line up, add or take away a st from row to make two sides symmetrical.
Rows 1–5 (7, 9, 12): tr/dc 5 (7, 9, 12) rows
Row 6 (8, 10, 13): Turn and dc/sc across end of sweater and down one side, sl st across underside of belly, sl st up opposite side of rump and tie off

DOILY APPLIQUÉ
Using 6.5 mm (K/10.5, 3) crochet hook, ch 3 and join in a ring.
Round 1: Htc/hdc 5 in ring.
Round 2: *Ch 2, sl st to join* and *repeat around ring.
Round 3: Sl st 1 up original ch 2 st, *ch 3 and join in middle of each ch 2* and *repeat around ring, tie off and sew in ends using a small hook or tapestry needle.
Using needle and thread sew doily appliqué to one side of collar.

Sweater Vest

For the preppy pup, this sweater vest keeps the torso warm and the body free to run and play.

Skill Level: Intermediate

Materials
Crochet hook size: 6.5 mm (K/3)
Yarn: Medium weight (4)
    Extra small,78m (85 yd)
    Small, 96m (105 yd)
    Medium, 105m (115 yd)
    Large, 119m (130 yd)

Gauge: 10 sts = 10 cm (4 in)

Special stitches
Bptr/bpdc: Back post treble crochet/Back post double crochet

Dimensions of finished vest

	Neck	Chest	Length
XSmall	23 cm	38 cm	25 cm
	(9 in)	(15 in)	(10 in)
Small	28 cm	43 cm	30 cm
	(11 in)	(17 in)	(12 in)
Medium	35 cm	56 cm	30 cm
	(14 in)	(22 in)	(12 in)
Large	41 cm	63 cm	38 cm
	(16 in)	(25 in)	(15 in)

Tip Increase the number of rounds between 2–6 to increase or decrease the length of the finished vest. When measuring make sure to leave sufficient room for male dogs to urinate.

Instructions are written for the Extra small size with Small, Medium, Large presented in brackets.

The pattern is worked from the chest up to the neck.

Ch 36 (56, 63, 69) and join in a loop.
Round 1: Ch 3, *tr/dc 33 (53, 60, 66), ch 3 and turn* ch 3 counts as first tr/dc for total 34 (54, 59, 65) tr/dc
Note: Ch 2 and turn after each round of bpo tr/dc and fpo tr/dc unless noted otherwise.
Round 2: *Repeat once.
Round 3: Bpo tr/dc 33 (53, 59, 65).
Round 4: Fpo tr/dc 33 (53, 59, 65).
Round 5: Bpo tr/dc 15 (26, 29, 32), dec 1, bpo tr/dc 16 (26, 29, 32).
Round 6: Fpo tr/dc 14 (25, 28, 31), dec 1, fpo tr/dc 15 (25, 28, 31).

EXTRA SMALL
Note: Ch 2 and turn after rounds and rows of fpo tr/dc and bptr/bpo unless otherwise noted.
Round 7: Bpo tr/dc 2, sl st 5, bpo tr/dc 13, sl st 5, ch 3, bpo tr/dc 2, and join, do not ch 3 and do not turn.
Round 8: Sl st 3, turn and ch 3, bpo tr/dc 5.
Rounds 9–10: *Ch 3 and turn, fpo tr/dc 5, ch 3 and turn, bpo tr/dc 5*.
Round 11–12: *Repeat.
Round 13: Sl 6 down side of chest piece, sl 5 across sl 5 gap (underleg), ch 3 and fpo tr/dc 12.
Rounds 14–15: *Ch 3 and turn, bpo tr/dc 12, ch 3 and turn, fpo tr/dc 12*.
Rounds 16–17: *Repeat.
Round 18: Bpo tr/dc 12.
Round 19: Do not ch 3 and do not turn, sl st 6 down back piece, sl st 5 across gap (underarm), sl st 6 up side of chest piece.
Round 20: Ch 3 and sl st to join with back piece, turn and sl st 9 (across ch 3 and across top of chest piece, ch 3 and sl st to join with other side of back piece.
Note: You have just created the two legholes.

Round 21: Turn and sl st 6, you are now at the centre of the front of the neck.
Round 22: Ch 3 and tr/dc around neck, sl st to join, do not ch 3.
Round 23: *Turn and sl st, dc/sc 1, tr/dc around neck, dc/sc in second to last st, sl st in last stitch of previous row, do not join*.
Rounds 24–28: *Repeat.
Tie off and weave in ends.

SMALL AND MEDIUM
Note: Ch 2 and turn after rounds and rows of fpo tr/dc and bptr/bpdc unless otherwise noted.
Round 7: Bpo tr/dc (24, 27), dec 1, bpo tr/dc (24, 27).
Round 8: Fpo tr/dc (23, 26), dec 1, fpo tr/dc (23, 26).
Round 9: Bpo tr/dc (4, 5), sl st 8, bpo tr/dc (24, 27), sl st 8, ch 3 bpo tr/dc (4, 5), do not turn.
Round 10: Sl st (4, 5), turn and ch 3, bpo tr/dc 9.
Row 11–12: *Ch 3 and turn fpo tr/dc 9 ch 3 and turn bpo tr/dc 9*.
Rows 13–18: *Repeat 3 times.
Row 19: Sl st 8 down side of chest piece and sl st 8 across underarm, ch 3 and bpo tr/dc (22, 24).
Row 20: *Fpo tr/dc across row (22, 24), ch 2 and turn, bpo tr/dc across row (22, 24).
Rows 21–24: *Repeat twice.
Row 25: Fpo tr/dc (22, 24) ch 2 and turn.
Row 26: Bpo tr/dc (22, 24), sl st 9 down side of back, sl st 8 across armhole gap, sl st 8 up side of chest piece, ch 4 and join to first st in row on back (you have now made the first armhole of the vest).
Row 27: Turn and sl st (12, 14) (across ch 4 and chest piece), ch 4 and join to the other side of the back (you now have two armholes).
Row 28: Turn and sl st (7, 9).
Row 29: Turn and sl st, dc/sc 1, tr/dc around neck, 1 dc/sc in second to last stitch, sl st next to starting sl st (centre of neck).
Row 30: *Turn and sl st, dc/sc, tr/dc around neck, dc/sc 1 in dc/sc stitch of last row, sl st in sl st of last row*.
Rows 31–36: *Repeat
Tie off.

LARGE

Note: Ch 2 and turn after rounds and rows of fpo tr/dc and bpo tr/dc unless otherwise noted.

Row 7: Bpo tr/dc 30, dec 1, bpo tr/dc 30.

Row 8: Fpo tr/dc 29, dec 1, fpo tr/dc 29.

Rows 9-10: Bpo tr/dc 58, fpo tr/dc 58.

Round 11: Bpo tr/dc 6, sl st 10, bpo tr/dc 26, sl st 10, ch 3, bpo tr/dc 6, do not turn.

Round 12: Sl st 6, turn and ch 3, bpo tr/dc 11.

Rows 13–16: *Ch 3 and turn, fpo tr/dc 11, ch 3 and turn, bpo tr/dc 11*.

Rows 17–24 *Repeat 4 times.

Round 25: Sl st 10 down side of chest piece and sl st 10 across underarm, ch 2 and bptr/bpo 26.

Rows 26–27: *Ch 2 and turn, fpo tr/dc 26, ch 2 and turn, bpo tr/dc 26*.

Rows 28–31: *Repeat twice.

Rows 32: Fpo tr/dc, dec 1, fpo tr/dc 13, ch 2 and turn.

Rows 33: Bpo tr/dc 25, ch 2 and turn.

Round 34: Fpo tr/dc 25, sl 10 down side of back, sl 10 across underarm, sl st 10 up side of chest piece, ch 5 and sl st to join with first st in row on back piece (you have now made the first leghole of the vest).

Round 35: Turn and sl st 17 (across ch 5 and chest piece), ch 5 and join to the other side of the back (you now have two legholes).

Round 36: Turn and sl st 11 (you are now at centre of front of neck.

Round 37: Turn and sl st, dc/sc 1, tr/dc around neck, dc/sc 1 in second to last stitch, sl st next to starting sl st (centre of neck).

Row 38: *Turn and sl st, dc/sc, tr/dc around neck, dc/sc 1 in dc/sc stitch of last row, sl st in sl st of last row*.

Rows 39–46: *Repeat.

Tie off.

With yarn B, dc/sc around top of collar and tie off, repeat on both armholes.
With yarn C, dc/sc around bottom of vest and tie off.
With yarn B dc/sc second stripe around bottom of vest and tie off. Weave in ends.

Sewing Projects

Heart

This felt heart also slides onto your pet's collar with an elastic loop, but could also be fitted with a clip on the back to attach to martingale collars. For a personal touch, embroider your pet's initial in the centre.

Skill level: Easy

Materials
1.5 cm (½ in)-wide elastic, 4 cm (1½ in)
Fabric glue
Felt: 22 x 28 cm (8½ x 11 in)
Scraps of contrast felt
Scraps of wadding (batting)
Fabric scissors
Needle and thread

Form the piece of elastic into a loop and use fabric glue to stick the ends together.
Using pattern pieces, cut two hearts from felt.
Cut one smaller heart from contrasting felt.
Cut a small heart from wadding (batting) slightly smaller than the small template.

Use fabric glue to stick the wadding to the inside of the back heart piece.
Sew the elastic loop to the back of the heart.
Sew the small heart accent to the front of the heart.
Place the front heart on top of the wadding and whip stitch the two halves together around the outer edge.

Bow Tie

This felt bow tie is perfect for attending the symphony or participating in some gentlemanly espionage. An elastic loop on the back of the tie slides over the end of your pet's collar to make this look as comfortable as it is classy.

Skill level: Easy

Materials
1.5 cm (½ in)-wide elastic, 4 cm (1½ in)
Fabric glue
Felt, 8½ x 11 in
Scraps of white felt
22 x 28 cm (8½ x 11 in) wadding (batting),
   6 mm (⅛ in) thick
Needle and thread

Form the piece of elastic into a loop and use fabric glue to stick the ends together. Using pattern pieces, cut two bow ties from felt and one set of bow-tie accents from white felt.

Cut the wadding slightly smaller than the bow tie.
Use fabric glue to adhere the wadding to the inside of the back bow-tie piece.
Sew the elastic loop to the back of the bow tie.
Use a needle and thread to stitch the accents into place on the front bow tie.
Place the front bow tie on top of the wadding layer of the back bow tie and whip stitch around the outer edge to join the two together.

Neck Tie

This simple tie is designed so that your pet's collar passes through a loop in the 'knot'. This project is very easy and perfect for kids to join in on the fun. Just cut out the template, fold, glue and decorate! Your pup will be ready for that high powered business meeting in no time.

Skill level: Easy

Materials
Red felt 22 x 28 cm (8½ x 11 in),
    plus scraps of two other felt colours
Fabric scissors
Fabric glue
Optional: glitter glue, buttons, embroidery
    thread or felt cutouts.

Photocopy the template provided,
enlarging it to fit your dog's collar Using
and cut out

Fold the piece of felt in half widthways. Place the top of the tie on the fold and cut out using fabric scissors. Stick the two halves together leaving a gap at the top to thread the collar through.
Cut out the decorations.
Stick in place as desired.

Bandana

The bandana is a classic doggy look, and this one slides on over the end of your pet's collar with no tying or bunching. The small triangle design has an opening for the collar to pass through, so there's no excess fabric or danger of it coming loose with wear. Try decorating your bandanna with embroidery, crocheted flowers, appliqué or fabric paint.

Skill level: Easy

Materials

Size	Fabric size	Fits neck
X small	15 x 15 cm (6 x 6 in)	18–25.5 cm (7–10 in)
Small	23 x 23 cm (9 x 9 in)	26–36 cm (10–14 in)
Medium	28 x 28 cm (11 x 11 in)	36–46 cm (14–18 in)
Large	34 x 34 cm (13½ x 13½ in)	43 cm + (17 in +)

Fabric scissors
Needle and thread
Chopstick or knitting needle

Cut one square from fabric. Turn in a small hem all around and press.

Fold in 5 cm (2 in) on two opposite corners and press.

Stitch the 5 cm (2 in) fold.

Fold the fabric in half, with wrong sides together to form a triangle, making sure that the folded corners are at each side of the widest part of the triangle.

Topstitch all around the triangle, leaving a gap at each side of the the fold to thread the collar through.

Upcycled T-Shirt Leash

Help your kids get involved with one of the most important responsibilities of pet ownership – regular exercise! This soft leash is created with recycled strips of t-shirts, and will provide kids with their own shorter leash to use when walking the dog. It is soft on smaller hands but strong enough to hold a pulling pup.

Skill Level: Easy

Materials
3 old t-shirts
Fabric scissors
1 metal leash clip in the size of your choice
 – we used a 4 cm (1½ in) swivel clip
Sewing machine
Needle and thread

Cut each t-shirt into one long continuous strip of fabric, which is 2.5 cm (1 in) wide and between 90cm–1.5 m (3–5 ft) long depending on the size of the child and the size of the puppy.

Gather the strips together and tie around a doorknob with a double knot, pulling each individual strip to tighten.

Using the doorknob to hold the fabric in place, plait (braid) the t-shirt strips together.

When you reach the end of the braid, thread one of the strips through the metal ring on the leash loop and knot. The t-shirt fabric is stretchy so if you pull each individual strip tightly and make a double knot, it provides a very tight hold. Trim excess fabric. To reinforce the leash you may choose to hand or machine stitch the base of the hand loop and the base of the leash loop for added strength.

Pet Silhouette Pillow

Bring your pet's adorable portrait into your décor in the form of a fabric silhouette. This unique appliquéd pillow honours your furry friend's one-of-a-kind face.

Skill level: Advanced
Finished size 30 cm (12 in) square

Materials
Fabric scissors
Light to medium-weight cotton, for the background, 1 m (yd)
Fusible interfacing (optional), 1 m (yd)
Computer printer and digital image or photograph of your pet in profile with the actual head to measure 16.5–19 cm (6½-7½ in)
Black cotton, for the silhouette, 25 cm (¼ yd)
Tracing paper and ballpoint pen
Fusible webbing with paper backing
Pins
Sewing machine
All-purpose thread
Seam ripper or tweezers
Wadding (batting) or pillow form
Pinking shears (optional)

Cut two squares each 32.5 cm (13 in) from the background fabric. If your fabric is lightweight iron fusible interfacing to the wrong side to stabilize it. Iron the fusible webbing to the wrong side of the contrast fabric, ensuring you protect the iron and ironing board from the glue on the webbing.

Resize the image of your pet profile to measure 16.5–19 cm (6½-7½ in) and print it out in black and white.

Use a ballpoint pen and tracing paper to trace the profile of your pet from the photograph or print out. Transfer the silhouette outline to the paper backing on the fusible webbing. Draw in the neckline freehand.

Cut out the head on the drawn line. Peel the backing paper off the fusible webbing. The web of glue will keep your fabric stable and help prevent fraying.

Centre the fabric sihouette glue side down on the right side of the fabric of the cushion front. Be careful not to put too many pins through the silhouette as the interfacing may make the pinholes more visible. A few pins along the outer edge will hold the fabric in place and will get covered by stitching.

Set your sewing machine to satin stitch, or use a wide zig-zag stitch with the stitch length set to 0.5. Begin sewing on the right side of your fabric, making sure the stitch encases the raw edge. Proceed slowly, raising your foot presser to go around curves. Make sure the needle is in the down position when raising the foot presser to keep a smooth outline.

When you return to the start point, backstitch about 6 mm (¼ in). Remove from the machine pull any thread ends to the back of the work, tie off and trim.

Pin the cushion front and back right sides facing, with raw edges aligned. Sew around the outer edge, using a 1.25 cm (½ in) seam allowance and leaving an 8 cm (3 in) gap at the base of the pillow for turning.

Turn the pillow right side out. Stuff the batting or pillow form in the gap base of the stitching, using a knitting needle or your finger to fill out the corners. Hand sew the gap closed.

Dog Coat with Crocheted Collar

Your buddy will be warm and cosy in this unique dog coat with crocheted collar. A small slit in the coat collar allows your pet's collar to pass through for a comfortable fit that's convenient for the walk.

Skill level: Beginner

Materials
Medium–heavy-weight fabric
    for the coat, 1 m (1 yd)
Lining, 1 m (1 yd)
5 cm (2 in)-wide strip of contrasting fabric for belt,
    65cm (26 in)
Scissors
Iron and ironing board
Co-ordinating sewing thread
6 mm (¼ in)-wide Velcro, 25 cm (9 in)
Pins

Crochet hook size: 6 mm (J/10)
Yarn bulky (5): 1 skein acrylic or cotton

Finished dimensions

	Neck	Chest	Length
XS	(10 in)	(16 in)	(9 in)
Small	(14 in)	(20 in)	(12 in)
Medium	(16 in)	(22 in)	(14 in)
Large	(18 in)	(24 in)	(16 in)

Gauge 12 sts = 4 in

SEWING THE COAT

Cut the fabric coat pieces using the pattern provided. Cut the same from lining.

Fold in and press 1.25 cm (½ in) on each side of the belt fabric to create a 2.5 cm (1 in)-wide strip. Pin the strip across the centre of the coat top. Top stitch along each long edge to create the belt at the waist.

Cut the Velcro into 7.5 cm (3 in) strips. With right side of lining facing you, arrange the Velcro loops horizontally according to the pattern piece on the left side of the collar and belt. Pin and stitch in place.

With right side of coat facing you, arrange the Velcro hooks vertically and pin onto the left side of the collar and belt. Pin and stitch in place.

Pin the coat and lining pieces together with right sides facing.

Stitch in place leaving a 10 cm (4 in) opening in the neck of the coat for turning. Turn the coat right side out using a knitting needle to turn out the straps. Top stitch around the outside of the coat, sewing the 10 cm (4 in) gap closed.

CROCHETED COLLAR

Instructions are written for the Extra Small size with Small, Medium, Large presented in brackets. Ch 40 (50, 58, 62).
Rows 1–2: Tr/dc across row, ch 3 and turn.
Row 3: Tr/dc 2, ch 2 and sk 2 sts, tr/dc in next st, tr/dc in next st and across row, ch 4 and turn.
Row 4: *Dtr/tr across row, ch 4 and turn*.
Rows 5–8: *Repeat (at end of row 8 ch 3 and turn).
Row 9: Tr/dc across row and tie off.
Weave in ends.
Pin crocheted collar to the outside neck edge of the coat. Top stitch in place. Reinforce the stitching.

Adjustable Dog Collar

Create a new look for your pet each season with this simple adjustable ID collar design. Buckles can be found at most fabric stores and curved comfort buckles and a wide variety of other decorative collar fittings can be found online.

Skill level: Intermediate

Materials
Tape measure
2.5 cm (1 in)-wide nylon, cotton or hemp webbing

	Webbing	Neck size
XSmall	48 cm (19 in)	15–25cm (6–10 in)
Small	61 cm (24 in)	28–36cm (11-14 in)
Medium	71 cm (28 in)	36–46cm (14-18 in)
Large	81 cm (32 in)	46–56cm (18-22 in)

Cigarette lighter or fray prevention glue
4 cm (1½ in)-wide strip of cotton fabric, 1 m (1 yd), or for small pets use 2 cm (¾ in)-wide ribbon
2 cm (¾ in)-wide strip of medium-weight fusible interfacing the same length as the cotton fabric
Iron and ironing board
Co-ordinating sewing thread
Sewing machine
Slide lock
Plastic buckle
D ring

Measure your pet's neck circumference and add 30 cm (12 in) to your measurement. Cut one length of webbing to your measurement.
Seal the edges of the webbing using a cigarette lighter. The flame will melt the webbing and stop it from fraying. Alternatively dab the raw ends with fray prevention glue.

Cut the cotton fabric the same length as the webbing and fuse the interfacing to the centre of the wrong side. Centre the fabric on the webbing and sew along each long side using the sewing machine. With right side facing the slide lock, pull the webbing up and back around the middle bar in the slide lock, leaving around 5 cm (2 in) on the end. Stitch in place with two seams and use the reverse button to reinforce the seam with a triple stitch.

Making sure the fold on the webbing is facing outward, thread the webbing through the side of the plastic buckle with just one opening (the female end of the buckle).

Next thread the webbing through the slide lock to create the adjustable part of the collar.

Slide the D ring onto the other end of the webbing. Slide the webbing through and around the other (male) side of the buckle, leaving 5 cm (2 in) on the end.

Sew a seam along the webbing as close to the buckle as you can, triple reinforcing the seam. Then pull the D ring as close to the seam as possible, and sew a second seam along the side of the D ring.

Leash Bag

It's never fun to find yourself without a bag when your pup decides to do their business. This small pouch conveniently attaches to your leash or belt loop and can hold 2-3 plastic bags or a small roll bags for the walk. Don't forget to include a few treats for training!

Skill level: Intermediate

Materials
Fabric scissors
Scraps of heavy-weight interfacing
Light-weight cotton fabric, 2 pieces each
    13 x 18 cm (5 x 7 in), for the bag
Iron and ironing board
Sewing machine
Sewing cotton
Pins
6 mm (¼ in)-wide cotton elastic, 20 cm (8 in)
Metal grommets
Metal key ring
Fabric handle.

Cut two squares of interfacing, each 1.25 cm (½ in). Place one interfacing square on the wrong side of one piece of the bag, placing it 5 cm (2 in) from one short edge (the bag top) and aligning raw edges with the **right**-hand long bag edge. The interfacing reinforces the fabric at the point where the eyelet (grommet) is positioned. Place a second interfacing square 5 cm (2 in) from one short edge (the bag top) and aligning raw edges with the **left**-hand long edge. Fuse both in place.

Pin the bag pieces right sides together and sew around two long sides and the bag bottom, beginning and ending 4 cm (1½ in) from the bag top and reinforcing the start and finish points by oversewing.

To make the casing for the elastic, press in a 6 mm (¼ in hem) at the top edge of the bag. Fold the hem down leaving a gap in the seam through which to thread the elastic. Stitch the turning in place creating a channel around the bag top.

Attach a safety pin to the elastic and feed through the seam opening and the channel.

Pull the elastic so it is slightly tight and stitch the raw edges together.

Position the eyelets following the manufacturer's instructions.

Turn the bag right side out.

Feed key ring through both grommets and thread through a handle.

Templates

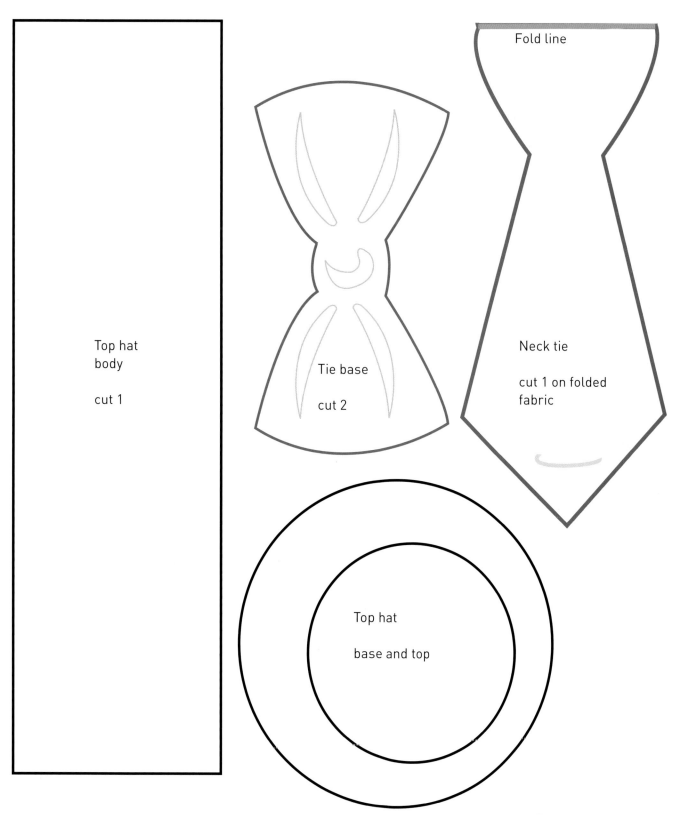

Top hat
body

cut 1

Fold line

Tie base

cut 2

Neck tie

cut 1 on folded
fabric

Top hat

base and top

Templates

Heart

cut 2 large hearts
cut 1 small heart

Under
belly
area

Tab

Dog coat

cut 2

Green = Extra small
Blue = Small
Black = Medium
Large = Purple

Enlarge 333% on a photocopier. You
will need to copy sections at a time
and stick them together. Stick the
pieces togehter and try the fit on
your dog. Adjust as necessary.

Neck

Rump

Tab

Tab